D1612709

WITHDRAWN
C334013648

Sacking
Aladdin's
CAVE

Plundering Hermann Göring's Nazi War Trophies

Kenneth D. Alford
with Thomas M. Johnson
and Mike F. Morris

Schiffer Publishing Ltd®

4880 Lower Valley Road • Atglen, PA 19310

Copyright © 2013 by Kenneth D. Alford

Library of Congress Control Number: 2013939096

All rights reserved. No part of this work may be reproduced or used in any form or by any means—graphic, electronic, or mechanical, including photocopying or information storage and retrieval systems—without written permission from the publisher.

The scanning, uploading, and distribution of this book or any part thereof via the Internet or via any other means without the permission of the publisher is illegal and punishable by law. Please purchase only authorized editions and do not participate in or encourage the electronic piracy of copyrighted materials.
"Schiffer," "Schiffer Publishing, Ltd. & Design," and the "Design of pen and inkwell" are registered trademarks of Schiffer Publishing, Ltd.

Type set in Magdeburg/LatinWidD/Minion Pro

ISBN: 978-0-7643-4396-4
Printed in China

Published by Schiffer Publishing, Ltd.
4880 Lower Valley Road
Atglen, PA 19310
Phone: (610) 593-1777; Fax: (610) 593-2002
E-mail: Info@schifferbooks.com

For our complete selection of fine books on this and related subjects,
please visit our website at **www.schifferbooks.com**. You may also write for a free catalog.

This book may be purchased from the publisher. Please try your bookstore first.

We are always looking for people to write books on new and related subjects. If you have an idea for a book, please contact us at **proposals@schifferbooks.com**.

Schiffer Publishing's titles are available at special discounts for bulk purchases for sales promotions or premiums. Special editions, including personalized covers, corporate imprints, and excerpts can be created in large quantities for special needs. For more information, contact the publisher.

In Europe, Schiffer books are distributed by
Bushwood Books
6 Marksbury Ave.
Kew Gardens
Surrey TW9 4JF England
Phone: 44 (0) 20 8392 8585; Fax: 44 (0) 20 8392 9876
E-mail: info@bushwoodbooks.co.uk
Website: www.bushwoodbooks.co.uk

Contents

Preface

In November 1862, Ambrose Burnside's Union Army encamped in Stafford Heights, on the east bank of the Rappahannock River, overlooking the town of Fredericksburg, Virginia. The Union fought here for six months in their unsuccessful campaign to advance further south and capture Richmond, the Capitol of the Confederacy. Located in the middle of Stafford Heights is Johnson Reference Books & Militaria, and it was here, at this historical sight, that the idea for this book originated.

In a meeting in Stafford Heights on a summer day in 2011, Thomas Johnson enlightened me, Kenneth D. Alford, that he had a friend with a detailed listing of the "Evaluation of the Majority of Gold and Silver items in Reichsmarschall Hermann Göring's Collection," which was a handwritten list of items stolen from the Hermann Göring Collection. The handwritten list had been purchased from Maude Anderson, the widow of U.S. Army Captain Harry V. Anderson. From previous books, I am most familiar with Captain Anderson, 101st Airborne Infantry, and his role in the safeguarding of Hermann Göring's massive treasure trove. Therefore I was skeptical, and told Johnson this just wasn't true. He disregarded my statement and suggested we write a book about this incident. I declined and returned home, but a dogged Johnson continued to try and convince me of the authenticity of this story. I believed this to be the biggest treasure find of World War II or a hoax.

I requested an e-mail of a couple of pages of the inventory, thinking that I could quickly debunk this story. Johnson's friend e-mailed me the questionable inventory pages and I spent two days analyzing the information by matching the inventory against the official inventory from Berchtesgaden, and then meticulously matched the documents against the property control cards from the Munich Collection Center. There were several matches. Now it became quite apparent that Anderson did indeed have an inventory of Göring's valuable silver and gold items, many encrusted with expensive gems. The list was a pencil record of the description of each item in a columned and lined German Brieftagebuch (daily journal or log book). The documents, written in English, was German influenced, as the values were in reichsmarks and there were many references to amber with the German word, Bernstein.

After six months of hard work, the story regarding the list did indeed prove to be a ruse, but not the inventory list. It was genuine. This list, along with many items, had been purchased on February 25, 1984, by Scott Merchant, of Round Rock, Texas, from Maude Anderson, living at the time in Austin, Texas. In the late 1980s, Texas collector Mike Morris purchased the bulk of most of these articles from Merchant. Somehow the inventory list took on a life of its own and became looted merchandise.

We had gone too far to turn back, and continued on with a fascinating straightforward story. The events in this book took place more than sixty years ago; therefore, all oral histories and statements have been double checked, for to shift from fact to fiction is a deceitfulness of historical accuracy. As with the previous book of the authors, *Sacking Aladdin's Cave* is related directly with one or more of our previous books, but a wealth of new research material has produced a masterful account of Göring's ill-gained war treasures.

1 $ = 2:50 R.M. (exchange rate of 1938)

Item	Type of metal	Einlauf / Description	Est. Value R.M.

Nr.	Empfang Jahr 19___		Abſender			Betreff	Beilagen	Bearbeiter	Bemer-kung
	Tag	Monat	Name uſw. und Ort	Dat.	Nr. oder Akz.				
1 Book silver	silver					signature book of the Goering		600 —	
1 Deer	silver gold plated					silver smith art with half gems		2200 —	
2 cups	bronze					metal art work		300 —	
1 light stand	silver 835 fine					big floor lamp		600 —	
1 desk 1 assembly	silver box + 3 disk assembly							250 — 150 —	
2 teapots 2 bowl	silver					antique silver work		1600 —	
1 teapot	silver					silver work		650 —	
1 Horse	bronze					market foundation		150 —	
1 Horse	bronze								
1 urn	silver					containing Rights defense law of 1938		150 —	

This is the first page of a list purchased from Captain Harry V. Anderson's widow. The cover page is titled "Evaluation of the Majority of the Gold and Silver items in the Göring Collection." *Courtesy of Mike Morris.*

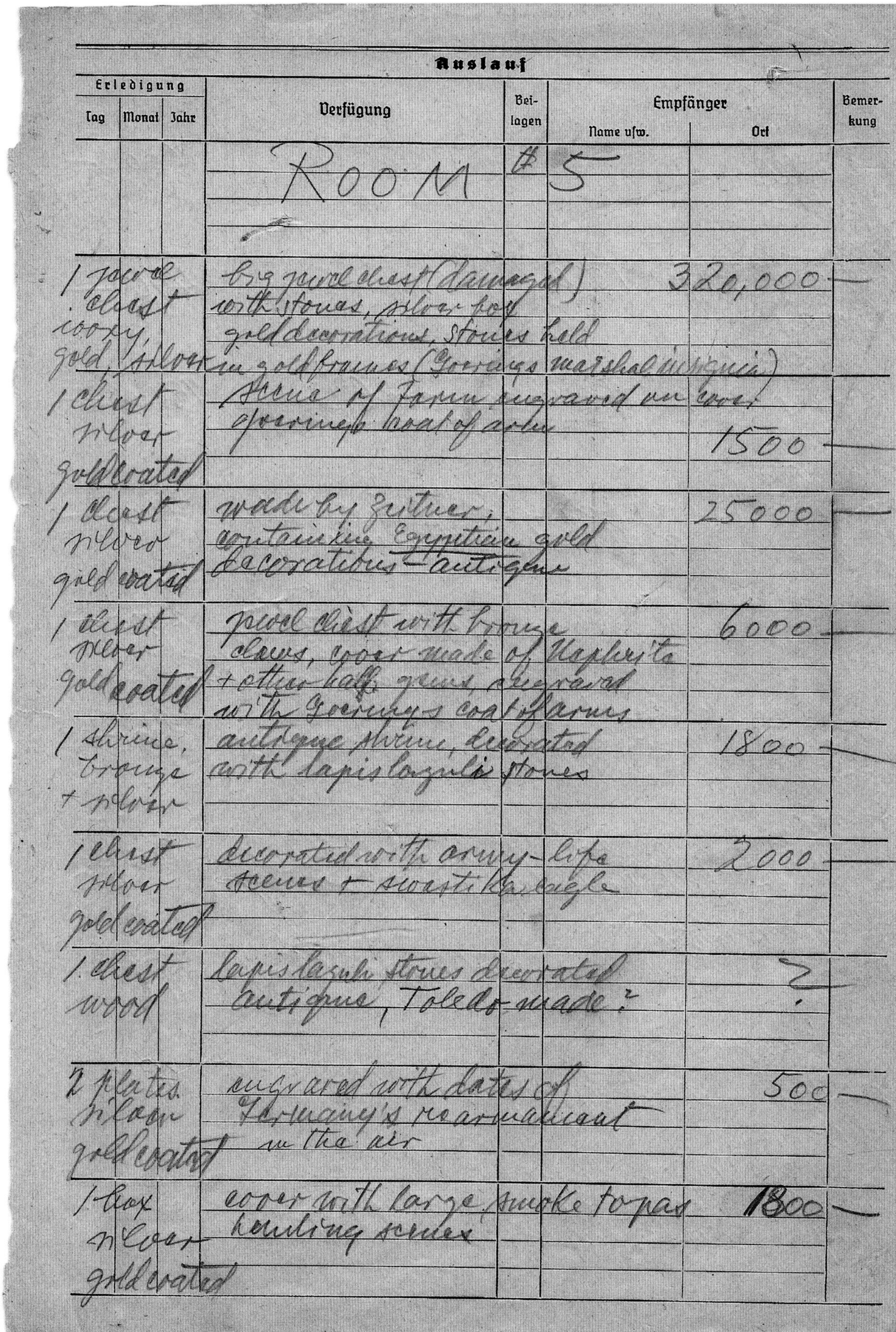

Auslauf

Erledigung: Tag / Monat / Jahr	Verfügung	Beilagen	Empfänger: Name usw.	Empfänger: Ort	Bemerkung
	ROOM #5				
1 jewel chest copper, gold, silver	big jewel chest (damaged) with stones, silver top gold decorations, stones held in gold frames (Goering's marshal insignia)			320,000	—
1 chest silver goldcoated	Scene of farm engraved on cover, Goering's coat of arms			1500	—
1 chest silver gold coated	made by Zeitner, containing Egyptian gold decorations – antique			25000	—
1 chest silver gold coated	jewel chest with bronze claws, cover made of lapislazuli + other half gems, engraved with Goering's coat of arms			6000	—
1 shrine, bronze + silver	antique shrine, decorated with lapislazuli stones			1800	—
1 chest silver gold coated	decorated with army-life scenes + swastika eagle			2000	—
1. chest wood	lapislazuli stones decorated antique, Toledo-made?			?	
2 plates silver gold coated	engraved with dates of Germany's rearmament in the air			500	—
1 box silver gold coated	cover with large smoke topas hunting scenes			1800	—

The inventory first page of room five, with the highest valued item at the top of the page – 1945 value $128,000. This was an unrealistic value, as the higher valued item auctioned in 1974 sold in the $5,000 range. *Courtesy of Mike Morris.*

Dr Matthias Weniger, Bayerisches Nationalmuseum; Dr. Hanns Löhr, Berlin; Allison Frew & Michelle Hevron, Virginia Museum of Fine Arts; and Captain James H. Page & John E. Foley, Pratt Museum, Fort Campbell, Kentucky. A special thanks to Ben Curtis, Texas.

Acknowledgment

Introduction

World War II – the bloodiest ever fought – was a global military conflict that, in terms of lives lost and material destruction, was the most devastating war in human history. The pillage from this war was not a departure of human greed, but merely a continuation of valuable objects seized from previous sacred and religious crusades during periods of hostilities. But during this conflict, Nazi plunder was to be exceptional in its scale and ruthlessness. The most flamboyant member of this Nazi hierarchy and object of continuing attention was none other than Reichsmarschall Hermann Göring, who added titles almost as frequently as he added new uniforms to his wardrobe.

The Nazi regime and ideology will be examined repeatedly by historians as one of the great phenomena of our time, and the psychological elements are so prominent that for those studies every possible resource and ample detail are certain to be required. *Sacking Aladdin's Cave: Plundering Hermann Göring's Nazi War Trophies* is not a book about the great battles fought during World War II or the Soviet Trophy Brigades, but it scrutinizes this evil regime through the opulent lifestyle of the loyal paladin of Adolf Hitler, Hermann Göring.

Following World War I, this disgruntled hero, who had been awarded Germany's highest honors, returned to Germany, which was struggling to regain stability after the devastating war and had little interest in giving any attention to an air hero from a bygone era. Depressed and drug addicted, Göring's fortunes rebounded, as he was closely tied to the rise of the National Socialist Worker's Party.

After Hitler was appointed Chancellor in 1933, the ruthless and energetic Göring created himself into the image of a political asset for the Nazi Party and the Third Reich. As president of Prussia, he created the Gestapo and established the concentration camps as he captured the hearts of the German people by bringing the mortal remains of his first wife from Sweden to his 100,000 acre domain just north of Berlin, Carinhall. He further endured himself to the people by a public wedding to his second wife, Emmy Sonnemann. All of this was captured in photographic detail by the German press and graced the image of the Reichsmarschall.

Göring's vaunted Luftwaffe enjoyed great success until the Russian winter crisis of 1941/42. This failure began to tarnish Göring's image with Hitler, but he still remained a favorite with the German populace. The last two years of the war Göring lived in semi-retirement, hunting, collecting stolen art, amassing trophies and awards, and designing fancy uniforms. In 1945, Göring fled the Berlin area with trainloads of treasures for the Nazi alpine resort in Berchtesgaden. Here the concentration of our research comes together concerning the dispersal of the Reichsmarschall's Nazi war trophies.

Reichsmarschall
HERMANN GÖRING

Reichsmarschall
Hermann Göring in
uniform with his prized
decorations and diamond
encrusted baton,
signifying his authority
and important position.
*Courtesy of Johnson
Reference Books &
Militaria.*

1

Reichsmarschall Hermann Göring

The son of a former governor of German Southwest Africa, Hermann Göring was born on January 12, 1893, in Rosenheim, Bavaria. Dr. Heinrich Ernst Göring, Hermann's father, had been a reserve officer in the Wars of 1866. In the early 1880s, his first wife died shortly after the birth of their fifth child. Heinrich, then serving as a County Court Judge, was appointed the Reich Commissar for the German Colony of South-West Africa by Chancellor Otto von Bismarck. In 1885, prior to leaving for his appointment in Africa and at the age of 46, Heinrich married 19-year-old Franziska Tiefenbrunn, known as Fanny. They traveled to Africa, and a year later she gave birth to Karl Ernst, who was delivered by a plump, mustached doctor named Ritter Hermann von Epenstein, an Austrian Jew. In this discomforting and deadly climate, three years later, Fanny gave birth to a girl, Olga, delivered again by Dr. von Epenstein. In 1890, after almost six years of service, the Göring family had to leave this African colony for health reasons.

After a long holiday recouping in Germany, Heinrich, Fanny, and their three children traveled to Haiti for his next assignment as the Resident Minister. Here ants bored their way through the floor of the kitchen and plagues of scorpions invaded their home. As a diversion from these annoyances, Fanny, an expert rider and huntswoman, took part in many organized activities accorded to the wife of a diplomat. Two years after arriving in Haiti, Fanny was expecting her fourth child. During these years she had maintained a steady correspondence with Doctor Ritter Hermann von Epenstein, and he advised Fanny to return to Germany for the birth of this child. Under his influences, she returned to Germany in October 1892, and on January 12, 1893, her fourth child was delivered by none other than Dr. von Epenstein. Fanny named the boy Hermann, after von Epenstein, who shortly afterwards announced that he was the Godfather of Hermann Wilhelm Göring.

Ten weeks after Hermann's birth Fanny returned to Haiti, leaving Hermann in the care of a Mrs. Graf, one of her closest friends. The family returned in 1896 when Hermann was three years old and took him with them to live in Berlin.

Upon reaching 60 years of age, it was mandatory that Heinrich Ernst Göring retire, which he did with a small annuity from the German government. Thus in 1898, due to a lack of money, the family had to leave Berlin. Here Hermann's Godfather came through, and the family moved to von Epenstein's Veldenstein Castle, Neuhaus, Bavaria. Fanny shared the bedroom with von Epenstein when he visited the castle, as the eligible bachelor traveled constantly. Hermann spent his childhood years living mostly in Veldenstein Castle, but spent many summers and Christmas holidays at von Epenstein's Mauterndorf Castle in Austria. Using von Epenstein's financial backing, the young Hermann Göring lived an affluent lifestyle and attended the most prestigious schools, graduating from the military academy in nearby Gross Lichterfelde.

In January 1914, 21-year old Hermann Göring joined the infantry regiment of Prince William as a lieutenant. Seven months later, after the outbreak of World War I, Göring was awarded the Iron Cross of the Second Class. In the beginning of the war Göring was an infantry officer; then, in the autumn of 1915, he passed his examination as a pilot. After 20 victories in the air, involving several hundred air battles, Göring was awarded Germany's highest decoration, the *Pour le Merite*. On July 7, 1918, Hermann Göring was appointed commander of the Manfred von Richthofen (the Red Baron) Super Squadron.

After the war Göring, like most German heroes, was unemployed and impoverished. Göring had several jobs that were airplane related, mainly from connections with his World War I associates. He sold parachutes and performed in air shows in Scandinavia. Here, in 1920, he met Carin von Kantzow, his future wife. A most attractive woman, she was married, and thus they carried on a scandalous affair. In 1922 Göring returned from Sweden, joined the Nazi party, and became Hitler's bodyguard. Meanwhile Carin had traveled to Munich, married Göring, and they lived quite lavishly from Carin's family money. They both admired and reveled in Hitler and his Nazi Party activities. Wounded in the groin during the beer hall putsch of November 1923, Göring became addicted to morphine that was given to ease his pain, and for several years was treated for this addiction. A wanted fugitive in Germany, he lived for about a year in Italy, living off his fame of World War I and occasionally money from Carin's mother. They returned to Sweden, where they lived frugally and sold off all their furniture and belongings just to survive. Göring was treated for morphine addition and Carin was in ill health, with both lung and heart problems. Frail for several years, Carin died just as Göring's star began to rise in the Nazi Party. She was buried in the family plot not far from Stockholm.

On November 6, 1932, Göring was elected Reichstag deputy, and then elected President of the Reichstag as a representative of the Nazi Party. On January 30, 1933, at 11 a.m., Adolf Hitler and Göring entered the Palace of the Reich, home of Field Marshal Paul von Hindenburg. When they entered, 10,000 hands were extended towards them with the Nazi salute. While minutes dragged along, suddenly Göring came out of the Palace, his face aglow, and he shouted triumphantly "Hitler has been appointed Chancellor of the Reich." "The Führer is Chancellor" cried the people, embracing one another and shaking hands while tears of joy flowed down their cheeks. The gate of freedom had been stormed and opened for the German people.

Göring was immediately appointed Minister of the Interior of Prussia, becoming President of Prussia three months later. From this power base he established the Nazi system in Prussia. In January 1933, Göring was also appointed Reich Commissioner for Aviation (Luftwaffe). To Göring himself, his greatest accomplishment was his appointment as the Master of the German Forests and Master of the German Hunt. In Prussia he appointed himself Forester of the former Prussian king's Rominten hunting preserve, some 60 thousand acres of woodland and meadows. He reorganized the hunting laws of the Greater Reich by requiring a hunting license and established a quota. Göring had a law passed forbidding vivisecting animals, hunting on horseback, and using wire or claw traps. By today's standards he would have been judged an environmentalist of great imagination and accomplishments.

Göring felt entitled to a sanctuary befitting his position as the second man in command of Nazi Germany. Therefore, in 1933 Göring acquired a country estate with a hunting lodge about 60 miles north of Berlin. The estate was a thousand acres that had been a state park with a hunting lodge near the center. The park was furrowed and covered with pine and oak trees. The estate was to be a symbol to the memory of his late wife and also serve as a monument to the Nazi regime and Göring himself. In 1934, Göring had his former wife's coffin removed from Sweden and entombed at the newly-named lodge, Carinhall. The swastika-draped coffin was carried by a train that stopped in the towns so mourners could pay their respects. The internment at the mausoleum was attended by Adolf Hitler and other Nazi dignitaries.

At Carinhall, named after his deceased wife, Baroness Carin von Kantzow of Sweden, Göring displayed his collection of art on all the walls and above the doorways. *Courtesy Library of Congress.*

Carinhall, Göring's country estate, began as a modest log cabin, but was transformed to be suitable to its owner. This palatial hall was used to entertain and impress his guests. *Courtesy Library of Congress.*

The Führer, ruler of the Third Reich, gave Emmy Göring this *Portrait of Bismarck* as a wedding present. The painter was Franz von Lenbach, her favorite artist. Otto von Bismarck was the ruler of the Second Reich. The First Reich was the Holy Roman Empire. *Courtesy National Archives.*

April 10, 1935, was the social event of the Third Reich, the wedding of Hermann Göring and Emmy Sonnemann. After an intimate relationship of two years, the actress Emmy was to become Göring's second wife. They were first married in a civil ceremony at Berlin City Hall. From City Hall to the cathedral, the streets were lined with flowers and guarded by Luftwaffe guards. As they were driven in two cars from City Hall to the cathedral, fighter aircraft flew over the city, roaring their approval of the marriage. At the cathedral, the wedding was blessed by the Nazi Reich Bishop of the Evangelical Church, Ludwig Müller. After the ceremony they were driven to Carinhall, where Göring prayed in the mausoleum containing Carin's remains.

Göring gave his bride a tiara of amethysts and diamonds while they received many expensive items. Hitler's gift to Emmy was a portrait of Bismarck. Göring received a most elaborate wedding sword from the Luftwaffe. The gifts from businessmen, municipalities, organizations, and museums had been carefully selected, as they had been notified in advance as to what presents Göring would enjoy receiving.

Göring's current political position gave him great economical power, and power corrupts absolutely. Göring's corruption and megalomania were exacerbated by his manic obsession for collected works of art, elaborate uniforms, and bejeweled objects. He craved the lifestyle that he had as a child while supported by his Godfather, Hermann von Epenstein. He was able to obtain this lifestyle via elaborate gifts he received for Christmas, New Years, and 12 days later on his birthday (January 12). He also obtained gifts of large sums of money throughout the year. All of this became accepted as doing business with the Nazi Party.

In 1936, the log cabin at Carinhall underwent a massive construction with an enormous new wing: the Hunting Hall, which was used for receptions for such U.S. dignitaries as former President Herbert Hoover and famed flyer Charles Lindbergh. Here each year on November 3rd, Göring celebrated the Feast of Saint Hubert, the patron saint of hunters. Carinhall expanded year by year and included a large basement with a gymnasium, lighted swimming pool, cinema, and game room. Here Göring practiced his marksmanship by shooting at moving animals projected on the walls. During Germany's darkest days during World War II, Göring's greed and vanity came through, as he continued to realize his ambitions by extending every luxury of stone, metal, and timber into the expansion of Carinhall.

The most exciting event in Berlin during the Third Reich was the annual Opera Ball that Göring organized on his birthday in 1936, and continued until the defeats in the war years. To be excluded from the invitation list was a social embarrassment, and the Nazi leaders eagerly awaited an invitation. The ball was modeled after the imperial balls of the royal families, with Prince and Princess zu Wied, Prince August Wilhelm, and other noble titles sanctifying the noble occasion. The zu Wieds gave their presence and little more, as their gifts were usually a box of schnapps, and one entry notes that one bottle was kaput.

The following year for New Years, Göring received an old powder horn as a gift from the Reich Hunting Office, a bronze deer from the seventeenth century, a hunting horn shrouded lamp, a book on hunting and proper forestry, a silver letter opener with animal sculpture, and from General Sepp Dietrich, hunting knives made by Heiden of Munich.

These gifts exemplify the presents Göring received due to his position as Master of the German Forest and Hunt. He had been a hunter for many years and devoted himself to this ancient German sport. *Courtesy National Archives.*

Göring is credited with the preservation of the elk and buffalo that were almost at the point of extinction. The bronze bison (right) was given to Göring by Minister of the Interior Wilhelm Frick as a Christmas gift in 1937. These valuable items were turned over to the Bavarian State in 1951. *Courtesy National Archives.*

Göring's gifts made up most of his art collection, but money was the most frequent gift that he received. Second on his gift list in popularity were flowers and floral arrangements. Azaleas were the trendiest gift, and even the Führer gave Göring a large azalea bush as a New Year's gift in 1937. He received silver and gold sculpture with gems in the shape of azalea bushes and flowers. Next were candlesticks and candelabrum by the hundreds, all shapes and sizes in bronze, gold, silver, ivory, and antlers. Silver cups and presentation plates by the hundreds, along with a jeweled chest, all made up the bulk of the *objets d'art* presented to Göring.

How do we know what Göring received? His staff was instructed to record every gift, such as the 177 items from his Christmas list of 1937. His 50th birthday list of January 12, 1943, contains 32 typed pages of gifts. The list was then redefined and typed in a category containing the 64 gifts received from the Nazi Leaders of the Third Reich. SS General Joseph "Sepp" Dietrich was most attentive with hunting daggers. The German Fishery gave a porcelain replicating a fish trawler, and several fish-shaped serving bowls. Gauleiter Julius Streicher did

Heinrich Knirr recreated this portrait in 1935 from a Heinrich Hoffmann photograph. Hitler was most pleased with Knirr's work, and only sat for one portrait painted by Knirr. This was a 1937 birthday gift to Göring from the Führer. This portrait was taken as a prize of war by the United States Army. *Courtesy National Archives.*

Hitler also presented Göring with this intriguing Hans Market, *The Falconries*, for his 45th birthday in 1938. This painting taken at Berchtesgaden was returned to Bavarian authorities in 1949, and it is today in the Neue Pinakothek in Munich. *Courtesy National Archives.*

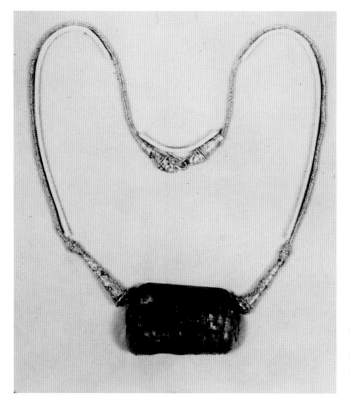

not enhance his standing with Göring by giving him two loaves of Nuremburg gingerbread for a 1937 Christmas gift, but then Streicher did not have to impress Göring. That same Christmas, Consul Willy Sachs, industrialist and German diplomat to Switzerland, gave Emmy Göring a motorcycle. Liquor, champagne, wine, and delicatessen items were also popular gifts from his household staff. For Christmas 1939, Göring listed cash gifts of 177,703.21 RM.

Every gift that Göring gave is also recorded by his staff for history. He gave his high ranking staff members a Christmas gift of 1,000 RM. Almost universally, he gave all staff employees the same: 10 cigars, 100 cigarettes, one bottle of wine, one large stolle, and 20 to 100 RM. It is interesting to note that at Carinhall in the later days of

Göring selected gifts from the Bornheim Art Gallery in Munich, and the gift would be paid for by the presenter. This large unidentified gem on a gold necklace was presented to Göring and came from this gallery. One birthday gift in 1940 from the Bornheim Art Gallery was a large painting *Leda* by the School of Leonardo da Vinci purchased at 150,000 reichsmarks by Gauleiter Koch. That same year the Luftwaffe purchased Göring a gift from Bornheim, a sculpture *Ritter St. George. Courtesy National Archives.*

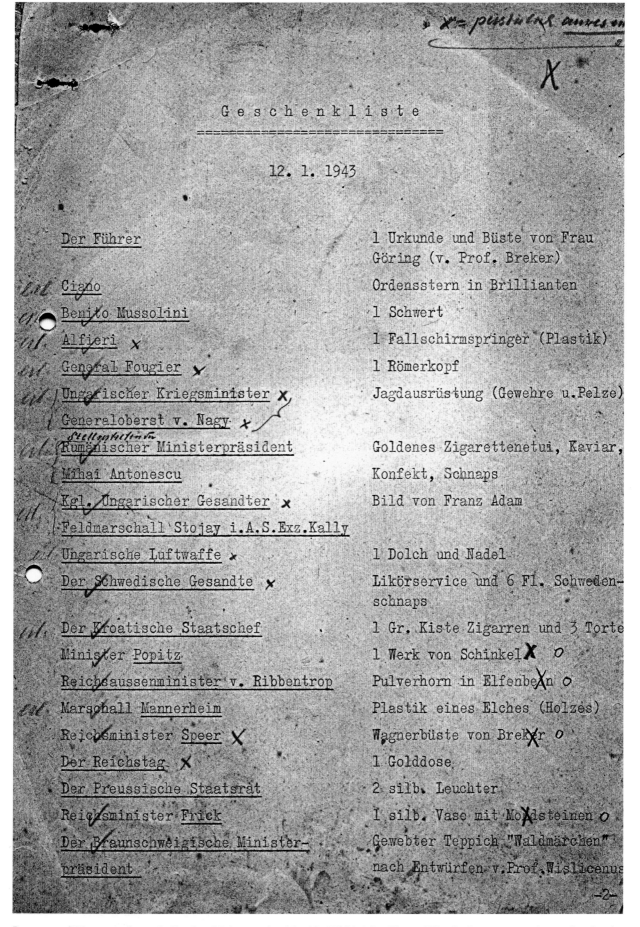

Geschenkliste
===============================

12. 1. 1943

Der Führer	1 Urkunde und Büste von Frau Göring (v. Prof. Breker)
Ciano	Ordensstern in Brillianten
Benito Mussolini	1 Schwert
Alfieri	1 Fallschirmspringer (Plastik)
General Fougier	1 Römerkopf
Ungarischer Kriegsminister	Jagdausrüstung (Gewehre u.Pelze)
Generaloberst v. Nagy	
Rumänischer Ministerpräsident	Goldenes Zigarettenetui, Kaviar,
Mihai Antonescu	Konfekt, Schnaps
Kgl. Ungarischer Gesandter	Bild von Franz Adam
Feldmarschall Stojay i.A.S.Exz.Kally	
Ungarische Luftwaffe	1 Dolch und Nadel
Der Schwedische Gesandte	Likörservice und 6 Fl. Schweden-schnaps
Der Kroatische Staatschef	1 Gr. Kiste Zigarren und 3 Torte
Minister Popitz	1 Werk von Schinkel
Reichsaussenminister v. Ribbentrop	Pulverhorn in Elfenbein
Marschall Mannerheim	Plastik eines Elches (Holzes)
Reichsminister Speer	Wagnerbüste von Breker
Der Reichstag	1 Golddose
Der Preussische Staatsrat	2 silb. Leuchter
Reichsminister Frick	1 silb. Vase mit Mondsteinen
Der Braunschweigische Minister-präsident	Gewebter Teppich "Waldmärchen" nach Entwürfen v.Prof.Wislicenus

-2-

Page one of 23 pages of typed gifts that Göring received for his 50th birthday. The red X = in the top corner is translated to be punctual. The blue X, along with the blue 0 markings, is unclear to the authors. *Courtesy of Mike Morris.*

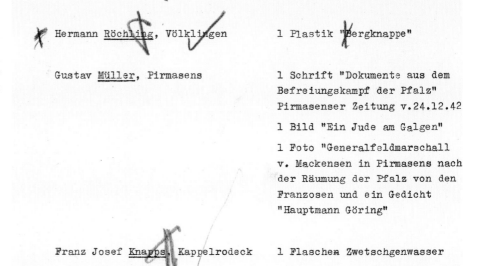

Supplementary page 21 of Göring's 50th birthday list. Göring's role in the Holocaust is replete, with his and his wife's help in assisting Jews during the war. The evidence of his ruthless criminal character comes to light with Gustav Müller's birthday gift: 1 Bild "Ein Jude am Galgen" (a picture of a Jew being hung). Who would give or receive a gift of a dead Jew, an intelligent, shrewd man or a tyrant gangster? *Courtesy of Mike Morris.*

the war the staff receiving gifts were the Fire Chief, three firefighters, and three camera men. At Mauterndorf Castle the staff receiving gifts included Master Hunter Harrer and his three assistant hunters, or Jäger. On Göring's staff were 18 people involved with only theater and film. His wife Emmy's annual Christmas gift of cash from Göring was 10,000 RM. Apparently in trouble during Christmas 1944, Göring gave 21 members of the Criminal Investigation Division money ranging from 50 to 300 RM. In typical German efficiency, he recorded each officer by rank and name.

On January 12, 1943, Göring celebrated his 50th birthday with an elaborate party, and also the most ornate gifts a conquering hero could acquire. On this celebrated day in frozen Russia, the powerful German Sixth Army was approaching a total of 750,000 killed, missing, or wounded in the brutal battle for Stalingrad. During this bloodiest battle of World War II, Göring and his guests were celebrating his birthday in the luxury of Carinhall. The guests had to have special gas rations in order to make the trip, while thirsty planes and tanks remained grounded for lack of fuel. The Sixth Army was encircled and surrendered because Göring had made serious errors of judgment in trying to supply Stalingrad with air support from the Luftwaffe. As this war progressed he lost prestige and influence with Hitler and the High German command, but surprisingly he did not lose popularity with the German public.

The ghastly war situation did not hinder Göring's celebration, nor the grandiose gifts that he received. Hitler gave Göring a certified bust of Emmy Göring crafted by noted German sculptor Professor Arno Breker. Next on the birthday list is Ciano's Star Medal with Diamonds, followed by his father-in-law Benito Mussolini's gift of an expensive and well crafted sword. It was to be a difficult year for both of these men.

Cortellazzo Ciano was an early supporter of Mussolini. On April 24, 1930, he married Edda, the daughter of Mussolini. Thereafter his promotions were very rapid indeed, as he was appointed Minister of Foreign Affairs, an office which he filled until February 1943. Shortly thereafter Mussolini was dismissed from office and arrested under orders of King Victor Emmanuel of Italy. Mussolini was rescued from prison on September 11, 1943, during a daring raid by Otto Skorzeny. He was reinstated under the puppet regimen of the Nazis that now occupied Italy as the Allies were fighting their way from the south of the Italian peninsula.

Mussolini then had Ciano arrested, tried, and found guilty of treason. He was sentenced to death, and the day before Göring's 51st birthday on January 11, 1944, at about 9:00 a.m. on a dreary dim cold day, five chairs with their legs were thrust into the ground. Ciano and four other men condemned for their role in the Grand Council vote to ouster Mussolini were ordered to sit down. They sat backwards in the chairs, as traitors were sentenced to be shot in the back. Their wrists were tied and they were executed. It took several shots to end the life of Ciano, dei conti di Cortellazzo.

Three more presenters of gifts for Göring's 50th birthday would witness the downfall of their country during 1944: the Ungarischer Kreigsminster, Kgl. Ungarischer Gesandter, and Ungarische Luftwaffe, which were the Hungarian Minister of War, Royal Hungarian Ambassador, and Field Marshall of the Hungarian Air Force, who gave hunting equipment that included a gun, a portrait by Franz Adam, and a high-quality dagger. As the mighty Red Army advanced toward Germany, Hungary, an Axis power aligned with Germany, deemed it appropriate to make peace. This led to Germany invading and occupying Hungary in March 1944. Otto Skorzeny played a major role in the overthrow of the then Miklós Horthy régime.

On this 50th birthday, Consul Willy Sachs, who had given Emmy Göring a motorcycle in 1937, gave Göring a Sèvres, 14 piece centerpiece of porcelain designed by eighteenth century Jean Baptiste Oudry, a French Rococo painter and engraver well known for his design of animals and hunting scenes. As Ambassador to Switzerland, Sachs had complete freedom to purchase art and send it back to Germany. He, like Göring, collected Lucas Cranach paintings. Then, at the end of the war, Sachs, a high ranking member of the Nazi Party, was arrested by American forces. His young attractive second wife, Ursula, took an American Lieutenant, Donovan Senter, as her lover. The

The Adam Franz painting *Before the Ride* was presented to Göring on his 50th birthday by the Royal Hungarian Ambassador. It had been seized from the M.W. Muzium Keptere in Budapest. It was turned over to the Bavarian State in 1949. *Courtesy National Archives.*

This 50th birthday gift, a silver gilded dish, contained the inscription "In the year 1942 in Witten the first synthetic butter was made from coal." The dish also contained a scoop of synthetic butter. The gift was given by A. Jmhausen, His name does not contain a red check mark on the birthday list which appears to be a sign to indicate a thank you note was sent. *Courtesy National Archives.*

Presented to Göring on his 50th birthday by the City of Berlin. This Tintoretto painting of *Diana* was purchased by Hofer in Italy with funds from Berlin. *Courtesy National Archives.*

Göring's staff had a Herculean task in removing the valuables from Carinhall. Here is Göring's large library filled with four walls of books. The two chandeliers lighting the room are seventeenth century and adapted for electricity. They were acquired for Carinhall by Alois Miedl, a German living in Holland with art and banking connections in that country. *Courtesy Library of Congress.*

The large office at Carinhall with a seventeenth century tapestry on the back wall. Again, this chandelier is identified as being from Holland. All of the heavy furniture in Carinhall was removed and taken into custody in Berchtesgaden by members of the 101st Airborne Division. *Courtesy Library of Congress.*

two of them stole most of Sachs' Cranach paintings and sold them in the Belgian black market art trade.

In late January, with the Allies advancing from the west and Soviet forces closing in from the east, Göring decided to move his collection away from Berlin to the south of Germany. He had his train, the Sonderzug, sent from Forst Zinna, near Jüterbog, north about 25 miles from Berlin. Attached to the train were six normal freight cars, three autopackers (freight cars for the transport of motor vehicles), and two French freight cars. The train continued on to Carinhall, and here Göring himself went through Carinhall with Walter Andreas Hofer and pointed out what he wanted to send immediately and what should wait for later transportation. Five of the normal freight cars were packed with treasures from the Kurfuerst bunker near Potsdam and Carinhall. The autopackers contained antique furniture, several large paintings, gramophone records, and the libraries of both Göring and Hofer. The two French freight cars were loaded with food. The dining car was loaded with the personal belongings of Generaloberest Loerzer and Göring's sister, Olga Rigele.

Göring's elaborate hunting room with a bearskin rug complete with the head, along with a decorative carpet running the length of the room. The room is completed with Italian antique tables and chairs purchased from Florence dealer Luigi Bellini. On one trip Göring purchased 74 large textiles and tapestries from Bellini. *Courtesy Library of Congress.*

In the skylight Festival Hall, the painting of the hunting scene on the left is unidentified. The marble column is from the Roman Empire. The Venus marble statue is second century Greek, and was a gift from Italian Air Marshall Italo Balbo. Following are a series of nine Flemish seventeenth century tapestries on loan from the Vienna Museum. For some unknown reason these tapestries were left behind by Göring and apparently recovered by Soviet Trophy Brigades. *Courtesy Library of Congress.*

This iron gate is a door to a stairwell leading to an upper floor. Across the top of the gate are four modern bronze figures. This is the upper end of a 100-foot corridor, one of many halls lined with paintings, tapestries, sculpture, and silver bric-a-brac. *Courtesy Library of Congress.*

According to Göring's art curator, Walter Andreas Hofer, they left several large size paintings in a storeroom, some of the heaver sculpture, such as a Greek Venus and some decorative garden pieces, along with sets of chairs and sofas. After their departure Göring had issued instructions for Carinhall to be dynamited. The engineers from Göring's paratrooper division had mined the house and Carin's mausoleum, and with the press of a button Göring's palatial palace was totally destroyed. No one could have guessed that the ruins were once one of the most ornate feudal residences in Germany.

On February 17, 1945, Hofer had the selected objects packed and they were trucked to the local train station, placed aboard Göring's special train (the Sonderzug), and sent to Neuhaus for storage in the Veldenstein Castle. The air raid shelter being built for this collection had not been

An ornate bronze door with a tiled hunting scene covers the floor. Four swords adorn the walls. Hermann Göring owned dozens of medieval swords that he used for decorative purposes at Carinhall, Veldenstein, and his other residences. The whereabouts of these numerous medieval swords remains unknown. *Courtesy Library of Congress.*

The reception room contains the valuable paintings and tapestries that were used for decoration throughout Carinhall. *Courtesy Library of Congress.*

Göring's private room, or his Gothic Room. The statue behind his desk is the Virgin Mary with baby Jesus and is from the early fifteenth century. The statue was purchased prewar by Walter Hofer. *Courtesy Library of Congress.*

In this room, a painting of Carin hangs on the left and Göring's current wife, Emmy, is featured on the right. Additionally, Göring had a portrait of Carin on his desk. *Courtesy Library of Congress.*

The portrait of Carin enshrined on the left wall was painted by Paraskewe von Bereskine shortly before her death at an early age. *Courtesy Library of Congress.*

This is the portrait of Emmy Göring mounted on the wall in the previous picture. It was painted in 1937 by Raffael Schuster-Woldan, Professor of the Prussian Academy of Fine Arts in Berlin. The frame is missing. Sometimes in moving the art from Carinhall to Berchtesgaden the frames were removed. The U.S. Army recovered several thousand empty frames from Göring's collection. *Courtesy Library of Congress.*

completed at Obersalzberg, and this is what necessitated the shipment to the castle. As a result, only the smaller *objets d'art* could be shipped because of the small rooms in the castle. Hofer traveled with the train, and upon arriving at Neuhaus station, had the objects unloaded onto trucks and stored in the castle according to special instructions sent down by Göring.

In March, many valuables were removed from the Kurfuerst shelter, loaded onto the special train, and journeyed to Carinhall. Here other valuables selected by Göring were packed with Hofer's help and sent to Veldenstein Castle. In early April, the third shipment containing everything that was left in the air raid shelter and most of what remained in Carinhall had been loaded onto one of Göring's special trains about 10 miles north of Carinhall at Vogelsang. At the last minute, an order was received that the train remain there until further notice. Hofer was instructed to travel to Veldenstein. On approximately April 5th, Fritz Goernnert appeared in Veldenstein with orders from Göring that all objects were to be packed and loaded onto the special train Sonderzug and await an imminent move. Some tapestries, sculptures, and paintings that had been in Veldenstein Castle were left there. After a week of waiting, the train was sent to Piding, 15 miles west of Salzburg. Here it made contact with the Verzug from Vogelsang. On April 16, 1945, the two trains crammed with valuables finally arrived in Berchtesgaden.

Upon arrival in Berchtesgaden they were parked in the train station tunnel. Hofer, who was in charge of the trains, lived in one of the cars. Thus, on April 12th all trains were together in Berchtesgaden. Göring's art treasures remained in the trains, which were pulled into the tunnel whenever the air raid sirens sounded. On April 30th, the trains were unloaded and the treasures were stored in a large unfinished air raid shelter situated along the road from Berchtesgaden to Koenigsee. The shelter was too small for the entire collection, so a day or two later one of the trains with eight baggage cars was sent to the village of Unterstein. The Allied Army was fast approaching Berchtesgaden.

In April 1945, Hitler gave Göring command of Southern Germany, and on April 23, 1945, Göring suggested he assumed power, as Hitler was trapped in Berlin. Hitler reacted furiously and had Göring arrested. He was in the hands of the SS until May 6, 1945, when he surrendered to the Americans.

Following the war, Carinhall was extensively searched by the Russians and later by the East German government. They blasted and dug large holes looking for art, tapestries, and sculpture. In 1991, a team on a moonlighting expedition excavated many art objects from the former underground Olympic-size swimming pool of the Reichsmarschall. This silver *objets d'art* was taken from the underground pool at Carinhall and is today in the collection of Mike Morris. The swastika hunting emblem is positioned between the solid silver stag's head. The insert is the engraved dedication "The Supreme Hunt Master of the Third Reich Hermann Göring in Great Admiration," signed September 1934. *Courtesy Mike Morris*

2
The 101st
Airborne Division

The 101st Airborne Division was organized at Camp Claiborne in 1942, under the command of General William C. Lee. While Göring was celebrating his 50th birthday, in 1943, the 101st Airborne Division was at Fort Bragg, North Carolina, training and organizing. By the end of 1943, the 101st would be in England, awaiting a rendezvous with Göring's treasured gifts. In his initial address, Lee stated that the 101st Airborne Infantry had no history, but a rendezvous with destiny. On that day no one could have guessed that the final rendezvous of World War II would include the distribution of Reichsmarschall Hermann Göring's wealth among the troops of the 101st in Berchtesgaden, Germany.

General William C. Lee, the father of the 101st, would not fulfill his mission of entering combat with the 101st, for on March 13, 1944, while stationed in England, he had a severe heart attack and was replaced by General Maxwell Davenport Taylor.

A native of Kansas City, Missouri, Taylor had been born there on August 26, 1900. He graduated from West Point on June 12, 1922, receiving a commission in the Corps of Engineers. In the mid-'20s he was in France studying French, and taught that language and Spanish at West Point until 1932. After that assignment he sailed to Japan and was stationed at the American Embassy as a student of the Japanese language. From there he was assigned to Beijing as a military attaché. As the war loomed over Asia, Taylor returned to the United States, and in July 1942 was assigned to Fort Bragg, as assistant division artillery commander. He shipped overseas, and in September 1943 was assigned to the Allied Forces Headquarters for duty with the Italian Military Mission on an assignment that would take him to Rome. At this time Italy was an Axis power with Germany, but aware of the turning tide of war, the Italian government was capitulating to the Allies, and Taylor was to help smooth the turnaround.

The journey began after midnight on September 6, 1943, as Taylor and Colonel William Gardiner boarded an Italian naval vessel and journeyed to an Italian port. Here they proceeded to Rome in an ambulance. Their mission was to prepare

The American eagle mascot of the 101st was the flesh and blood of the Division's Screaming Eagle shoulder patch. Unfortunately "Young Abe" never saw action with his outfit. He died in May 1943 at Fort Bragg while the division was on training maneuvers in Tennessee. Four months later the 101st began its ocean crossing to England. *Courtesy National Archives.*

for the drop of the 82nd Airborne Infantry Division into Rome, and with the help of the Italian Army hold that city against German advances. The Italian officials in Rome were less that enthusiastic to see Taylor. Under stress, Taylor forced a meeting with the Prime Minister, Marshall Pietro Badoglio. In the lateness of the night the 73-year old Minister met them in his pajamas. The Italian officials stressed in no uncertain terms that they could not support an Allied airdrop into Rome. The 82nd Airborne, without trucks, supplies, and ammunition from the Italians, could not survive. Taylor, realizing the improbability of the situation, radioed the Allies in Sicily to call off the airdrop into Rome. For this mission General Maxwell Taylor was awarded a Silver Star.

After several weeks Taylor returned to England with the 82nd Airborne Division. After Lee's heart attack, Taylor took command of the 101st Airborne Division on March 14, 1944, at its headquarters in Newbury, Berkshire.

General Maxwell Taylor, Commander of the 101st Airborne Division, distinguished soldier, statesman, and Presidential advisor. *Courtesy U.S. Army, Center Military History.*

3

Normandy

On the evening of June 5, 1944, the night was filled with the roar of countless engines. Tow lines stretched taut, the signal tower blinked take-off signals, and the first elements of a vast armada rose into the sky. When the lead echelons of aircraft reached the coast of France, a thick barrage of ack-ack blanketed the planes. Some gliders were forced to cut loose from damaged tow planes and crash landed into the English Channel. The flak was so dense the jump formations were broken, and sticks of paratroopers were scattered over a fifteen mile area, a factor that was to play a vital part in the success of the mission.

The majority of the aircraft flew inland, and in the early morning darkness of June 6, 1944, thousands of parachutists spilled from their bullet-riddled transports as gliders circled down through a bullet tracer and flak filled sky. Widely scattered jump and glider landings, plus stiff enemy resistance encountered immediately, prevented men from forming full units. Instead, isolated bands of mixed soldiers fought their way toward their military objectives.

The 101st Airborne was assigned a three-fold mission involving the capture of causeways leading inland from the invasion beaches and the destruction of bridges across vital German support roads. Instead of fully assembled units moving to these objectives, D-day found a wide area of the Cotentin Peninsula spotted with roving bands of artillerymen, infantrymen, ordinance, and cooks engaging the enemy at countless non-critical targets. Well briefed, the soldiers were not hampered by this unplanned dispersion of men. Trained to be individual fighters and schooled in the use of whatever weapons were available, the odd assortment of fighting men that roamed the hedge rows in the Normandy fields defeated the enemy in a successfully accomplished mission.

In the battle for Carentan, the 3rd Battalion of the 502nd Parachute Regiment, led by Lt. Col Robert G. Cole, was driving towards the city from the north. After crossing four consecutive bridges which span the Carentan waterway approaches and establishing a bridgehead, the Battalion was pinned down by heavy enemy fire. Lt. Col. Cole and the paratroopers flattened into the marshy

Paratroopers of the 75-mm howitzer section, 577th Field Artillery, 101st Airborne Division position their parachutes before loading into C-47 cargo planes in Newbury, England. *Courtesy National Archives.*

swamp for cover. After unceasing German fire had prevented any movement for more than an hour, Cole ordered a bayonet attack! He ordered "Strip for bayonet attack! Let's get out of this damn swamp." Here, on the last approach to Carentan, occurred the first bayonet attack of World War II by American troops. Locked in hand-to-hand fighting, the paratroopers forced back and subdued the German defenders. For his heroic action, Lt. Col. Cole was posthumously awarded the Congressional Medal of Honor. He was killed on the second day of fighting during the airborne invasion of Holland.

Of the men who flew across the English Channel, only about half returned between July 11th and 13th. The rest had been evacuated earlier to hospitals, or had been buried in France. The brilliant success of the mission was only accomplished with a great loss of life.

Back in England, the men of the 101st were given a brief rest, reequipped, and prepared for another mission. Newly arrived replacements took their place in the outfit, and the division moved again to marshalling areas, packed new parachutes on, and all but boarded the planes as the Third Army overran their objectives. But the next trip to the airfield was no dry run, and on September 17, 1944, the paratroopers took to the sky for drop zones in Holland for the important city of Eindhoven. The 101st was part of the First Allied Airborne Army, which was the largest mass of airborne troops and equipment ever assembled for an operation.

4

Market Garden

On May 10, 1940, the German Tenth Army, spearheaded by airborne troops, invaded the Netherlands. The rest of the Wehrmacht force, committed to overrunning Western Europe, executed their well planned invasion through Belgium and the Ardennes Forest. On May 14, 1940, the Dutch commander ordered a cease-fire. Three days later, the entire Netherlands was occupied by Nazi Germany.

The Nazis set up a puppet government and established a Dutch National Socialist Party. Some Dutch citizens eagerly joined the new Nazi party and took positions in the government. Others, however, joined with the purpose of pretending to collaborate while remaining loyal to the government-in-exile. Their positions enabled them to keep an eye on Dutch collaborators and to influence policy making and implementation.

As the harshness of the occupation grew, so did Dutch unrest and resentment toward the Germans. Individual Dutchmen took it upon themselves to strike back. With no central command, these brave individuals began recruiting relatives, friends, and neighbors into the first resistance organizations.

Members of the Dutch royal armed forces who had not escaped to Britain and had successfully evaded German capture secretly banded together and began collecting information. With the help of radio experts they established a wireless link with the British Secret Intelligence Service and began passing information to the Allies. The British Military Intelligence Section was set up to exploit these available resistance groups. The Military Intelligence Section infiltrated agents, usually by parachute, into occupied Holland and linked up with these resistance cells. They brought money, maps, and false papers.

Therefore, the Allies had an elaborate espionage network and an underground organization of some 1,500 saboteurs operating in German-occupied Holland – or so they believed. In actual fact, the "Underground" radios reporting back to London had been worked by six German operators using 17 captured British wireless radio sets. As early as 1942, the operation was penetrated by German counter-espionage under Major

Hermann J. Giskes of the Abwehr. Fifty-four London-trained secret agents sat in Mauthausen Concentration Camp while the German counter-intelligence manufactured fairy tales about these agents' activities to report to England.

Realizing that the 1,500 fictional men urgently needed supplies, the German operators radioed London for such articles as clothing, footwear, cigarettes, coffee, tea, plastic explosives, and penicillin. The plastic explosives were better than anything the Wehrmacht had, and penicillin was nonexistent on the Fortress Continent of Europe. At the arranged time a few cars with dimmed headlights parked in the woods near the drop zone, where three men with powerful red-beamed flashlights were standing, making up a large triangle. They heard the hum of aircraft engines and a plane swept overhead at hardly 600 feet. Heavy containers hit the ground as the plane gained altitude and blinked its navigation lights in a salute and disappeared. The agents could not believe their eyes, as the dropped consignment exceeded five tons. Unbelievable air drops came in on an almost conveyor belt schedule.

Again, to enforce their dependability with London, the German agents operating in Holland and now Belgium located a number of Allied flyers and guided them on an adventurous underground journey to the Spanish border. The flyers had absolutely no knowledge they were escaping under the protection of the Gestapo. The German agents would radio London with the names and ranks of the escapees, and when the flyers arrived in England, the prestige of the German based agents in Holland was greatly enhanced.

Using reliable British Military Intelligence Section information, the Germans completely infiltrated every major unit involved in the Dutch resistance. There is no evidence that the German deception was ever discovered by the Allies, but on April Fools Day 1944, the Germans discontinued their daily transmissions. This was one of the most gigantic hoaxes perpetrated on the Allies during the entire war, and during this critical time the Allies were using intelligence information from the Dutch resistance to plan for Operation Market Garden.[1]

The Battle

One of the most spectacular Allied offenses – Market Garden, conceived by controversial General Bernard Montgomery – began on September 17, 1944, as a great Allied airborne army of parachutists and glider men dropped out of the skies to land on Dutch soil and flank the Siegfried line defenses of Germany. The greatest massed airborne fleet ever assembled for an operation left airfields in England and flew a course over the English Channel, and while the first planes were spilling its parachutists and first gliders were coming to a halt on the low lands, the last planes and gliders were taking off from Britain's runways. Dropped behind enemy lines, three divisions of paratroopers were to be joined by massive armored columns breaking through from the south. The operation failed, as the units encountered vicious combat from the German defenses.

As part of this newly-formed Allied Airborne Army, the 101st Airborne division, under the command of Major General Maxwell D. Taylor, assembled at marshalling airdromes in Britain just a little over two months after leaving the combat areas in Normandy, where the Division had spearheaded the Allied invasion of Western Europe.

The parachute echelon of the 101st Airborne Division consisted of 436 C-47 transport planes carrying 6,809 parachutists. Four hundred twenty-four planes dropped troops on D-day and 12 planes carried the Parachute Field Artillery Battalion.

The drop was designed to lay a carpet of airborne troops along a narrow corridor extending approximately 60 miles into Holland from Eindhoven northward to Arnhem. The airborne troops were to secure bridges across a number of canals, as well as across three major river barriers. Through this corridor opened by the airborne, troops were to pass British ground troops in a prompt push to Arnhem. The principal objective of the operation was to get

Allied troops across the Rhine. Three main advantages were cutting the land exit of those Germans remaining in western Holland: outflanking the enemy's frontier defenses, the Siegfried Line, and positioning British ground forces for a subsequent drive into Berlin.

The supreme commander, Dwight Eisenhower, endorsed Montgomery's strategy and provided him General Lewis H. Brereton's First Allied Airborne Army. Later, he agreed to divert supplies from other fronts to Montgomery's Twenty-First Army Group, therefore setting the scene for one of the Allies' most disastrous errors in northwest Europe.

As the code name implied, the operation, commanded tactically by British Army officer Lieutenant General Frederick Browning, was divided into two phases: Market was the employment of airborne troops to seize bridges across eight water barriers; and Garden, the advance of General Brian Horrocks' XXX Corps across the bridges. Speed was essential, with Horrocks having to cover in three days the 59 miles to Arnhem from his starting line on the Meuse-Escaut Canal on the Belgian-Dutch border.

Part of a crew of a glider from the 101st Airborne Division who took part in the landing behind German lines in Holland pose beside their craft before take-off at an airdrome in England. *Courtesy National Archives.*

Parachute drop of the 101st Airborne in Holland. The chute in the middle contains supplies, with the stick figures of soldiers seen in the background. *Courtesy National Archives.*

Dutch civilians help 101st Airborne troops unload a glider after it landed in a turnip field in Holland. *Courtesy National Archives.*

To capture the bridges, the 101st U.S. Airborne Division landed between Eindhoven and Veghel, a fifteen mile stretch; the 82nd U.S. Airborne Division dropped further up the corridor around Crave and Groesbeek; and the1st British Airborne Division dropped near Arnhem, but not near enough as planned; due to rough terrain they were dropped 12 miles from their objective. The initial drop of 16,500 paratroopers and 3,500 troops in gliders was completed with unprecedented accuracy, but from that high point the tactical execution of Montgomery's bold strategy deteriorated.

It took four hours for British paratroopers to reach the bridge at Arnhem on foot, by which time German resistance was already stiffened. The railway bridge was destroyed and the British, their forces already scattered and pinned down by a stout German defense, were only able to capture the northern end of the road bridge. The final blow came when bad weather delayed reinforcement by the Polish Parachute Brigade. Some were dropped at Driel, across the river from Arnhem, but the Germans prevented them from crossing.

Stubborn German resistance also delayed the land forces. The XXX Corps was a day late when it linked up with the 101st Airborne Division near Eindhoven. The schedule called for British troops to be in Eindhoven within three hours of the 101st drop. Also, the construction of a Bailey bridge just north of Eindhoven at Zon, to replace one destroyed by the Germans, put Horrocks an additional 33 hours behind schedule. The advance of the British VIII and XII Corps on either side of the narrow corridor being carved out for XXX Corps was also, as Montgomery admitted, "depressingly slow," and their tardiness exposed the 101st Airborne Division to increasingly intense flank attacks which cut the Eindhoven-Nijmegen road known as Hell's Highway more than once.

On the second day of the drop, September 18, 1944, Private First Class Joe E. Mann, Company H, 502d Parachute Infantry, had encountered the enemy in the vicinity of Best, Holland. His platoon, attempting to seize the bridge across the Wilhelmina Canal, was surrounded and isolated by a German force greatly superior in personnel and firepower. Acting as lead scout, PFC Mann boldly crept to within rocket launcher range of an enemy artillery position and, in the face of heavy enemy fire, destroyed an 88mm gun and an ammunition dump. Completely disregarding the great danger involved, he remained in his exposed position and, with his M-1 rifle, killed the enemy one by one until he was wounded four times. Taken to a covered position, he insisted on returning to a forward position to stand guard during the night. On the following morning the enemy launched a concerted attack and advanced to within a few yards of his position, throwing hand grenades as they approached. One of these landed within a few feet of PFC Mann. Unable to raise his arms, which were bandaged to his body, he yelled "grenade" and threw his body over the grenade, and as it exploded, he died. PFC Joe Mann was awarded the Congressional Medal of Honor.

On September 25th, the British pulled back their surviving paratroopers from Arnhem to the Lower Rhine River for withdrawal that night. Although 2,163 men of the 1st Airborne Division and 160 Poles escaped, the Germans took more than 6,000 captive, nearly half of whom were wounded. The losses of the two U.S. Airborne Divisions, which stayed on the line for another two months, totaled 3,532.[2]

There were several reasons for the failure of Market Garden. The remains of two SS Panzer Divisions, the 9th and 10th, were refitting in the area of the Market Garden operations, and they had just completed an exercise on how to repel an airborne landing. Indications of their presence before the landings had been ignored. There was good reason for this, as the British spy network in the Netherlands had been thoroughly compromised, and the British assumed correctly that the Dutch resistance had been similarly penetrated. Therefore British intelligence took care to minimize intelligence information from Dutch sources.

A second underlying principle was the capture by the Germans of the complete operational plans for Market Garden. The plans were found in a Waco freight glider near German General Kurt Student's headquarters at Vught. This town was almost between the drop zones for the 82nd and 101st Airborne Divisions. It is commonly reported that in the Waco was the body of an American Army captain, and his undamaged briefcase contained the complete attack plans. With these secret documents in his possession, General Student moved anti-aircraft units, self-propelled guns, tanks, and infantry immediately to Arnhem. In Cornelius Ryan's excellent book *A Bridge too Far*, he footnotes "In any case … I think it highly unlikely that the entire Market-Garden operation plan could have been in the possession of a captain." Although he had written *The Longest Day*, Ryan was unaware that on the evening of D-Day, June 6, 1944, a copy of the VII Corps field order had been picked up by the German 914th Regiment from a boat that drifted ashore in the mouth of the Vire River (Seine Bay). The next evening a copy of the V Corps order was taken from the body of an American officer killed at Vierville-sur-Mer.

Oberstleutnant Fitz Ziegelmann wrote:

> The plan of V corps was taken off a youngish, U.S. Army officer, who had been killed in action on the late afternoon of 7 June '44, in the southern quarter of the village of Vierville, or rather, immediately to the East thereof.
>
> The dead officer was said to have had the plan with him in an ordinary briefcase. After receiving the plan I was personally of the opinion that the deceased officer must have belonged to the staff of the 29 Inf. Div, or of V Corps. The distribution of the plan, which covered 100 pages, did not reveal the identity of the owner. Personally I believe the dead U.S. Army officer to have been a member of an advance party of a staff (29 Infantry Division or V Corps).[3]

These three sets of documents contained the names of all the divisions employed in the attack, as well as the exact locations of drop zones and critical bridge and town objectives. These plans, captured by the Germans, clearly showed the methods and directions of the Allied Armies. They were numbered, and great care was taken in their distribution; surely they were accounted for on a daily basis. There is only a brief mention in official records of this tragedy that was responsible for the deaths of thousands of American, British, and Canadian soldiers.

On the other hand, General Robert E. Lee's plans for the invasion of Maryland were found by a Union soldier and passed into the hands of General George McClellan. In the aftermath of the Civil War this lost dispatch received extensive coverage. To this day, students of the Civil War argue the question of what happened and what the long-term implications were.

But no one discusses the implications of the plans captured by the Germans. Was the evidence burned in the destruction of the Criminal Investigation Division files? Surely these highly secretive and numbered missing papers were immediately investigated by a competent U.S. Military Intelligence agency?

Although the attempt to gain a bridgehead across the lower Rhine failed, the Allies retained a salient into Holland that went nowhere – a disastrous error indeed. But this courageous operation offered pillaging on a grand scale, as the locals had no advance notice of the military operation. They did not have time to hide valuables in a secret location. Therefore, the banks, post offices, town halls, and private safes were prime picking for the Allied invaders. Regarding the widespread looting in Holland, particularly the town of Heteren by members of the 101st Airborne Division, General Maxwell Taylor wrote:

> Due to the fact that irresponsible civilians as well as troops of various organizations – both British and American – were in and around Heteren during the period when the safes were opened, responsibility cannot be fixed with certainty, as opposed to individual culpability, there is no procedure by which the individual owners of the safes in Heteren can be reimbursed for damages suffered. I feel that such damages under the circumstances are in nature of property losses, which are inevitable concomitant of war.[4]

On November 28, 1944, after 72 days in Holland, the airborne forces were trucked to Camp Mourmelon, France, for rest and recuperation. After a thorough investigation by authorities of the 101st Airborne Division, three enlisted men were arrested for looting; one company commander was relieved and fined; and one company commander, three platoon commanders, and two battalion commanders were admonished for failure to take adequate measures to prevent looting.[5]

In the papers of the investigations it was written, "After all they were only picking up trophies and taking some wine from cellars."

But as we shall see later at Berchtesgaden, the soldiers of the 101st Division would amass a treasure trove of trophies.

5

Bastogne

astogne was a quiet village in the Belgian Ardennes, which would have remained a quiet village if it had not been for the fact that four highways met there. In 1940, the war had passed Bastogne quietly, this first time, and now the Americans had easily taken the town, and it was an American garrison for a quartermaster bakery. But in December 1944, the town became a priority objective when German Gerd Von Rundstedt launched Hitler's last offensive attack of World War II. For a brief moment the bakery was all that stood between the German Army and the Belgian port of Antwerp.

The 101st had just settled in the muddy base at Mourmelon-le-Grand, France, when the frantic alert for Bastogne was issued. The 73-day campaign in Holland had left the soldiers sparsely equipped, and the men wore a hodgepodge of uniforms as they boarded trucks a few hours after the alert order and headed for the Belgian Ardennes. Officers and men just returning from leave pulled on fatigue clothes over their dress uniforms, grabbed helmets and rifles and went along. One battalion was left in Paris on pass. The vast majority were without ammunition until it was doled out to them when they left the trucks prior to marching towards the front. On December 17th, the 101st pulled into Bastogne. The roads out of town were jammed with bedraggled troops and vehicles of several units. The scene was one of weary confusion. Someone asked an MP directing traffic at a road junction what was the situation and he replied with a shrug, "I don't know. Everyone else is leaving and the 101st is coming in."

On December 21st, the 10th Armored Division, along with the 101st, was swallowed in the red tide that was spread over the map. Bastogne was one black spot, like a hole in a big donut. For six days the 101st was completely cut off by savagely attacking elements of eight German divisions. An unending barrage of artillery and night bombings hammered Bastogne to rubble. Wounded men were sent back from the front, only to lie helplessly in a town under a continual rain of shell fire. Surrounded, evacuation was impossible. Doctors and technicians were captured when the division aid station was overrun, which put an added burden on the already overworked and under-equipped medical men. One hospital suffered a direct bomb hit – no patient survived. German Radio Berlin reported the 101st as annihilated. Enemy forces at first routed division units from hastily built defenses north of Bastogne. Part of the 506th entered Noville and was pounded mercilessly by direct fire from guns on the hill around the town. Swarms of enemy tanks and men overran the undermanned positions of the defenders and the front lines wavered dangerously. The tacticians of the 101st were accustomed to encirclement and learned to cope with it. Battle toughened troops used to fighting behind enemy lines in Normandy and Holland organized their defense of continuous attack in all directions. Another enemy, General Winter, sent his legions into the battle. Trench foot and frozen limbs matched casualties from artillery and small arms. Men fashioned crude jackets from blankets and tarpaulins and made scarves from supply parachutes. Even cooks and clerks left their typewriters for guns, filling gaps in a depleted line. Tenaciously they clung to frozen slopes and stiff limbed piles of German corpses that littered the ground in front of their position.

Four Germans under a white flag delivered a surrender demand to the garrison. Acting Division Commander General Anthony C. McAuliffe tersely answered "Nuts." A corps of enemy artillery was supposedly waiting to level the town. The men of the 101st chipped deeper into the frozen earth, smiled grimly at McAuliffe's reply, and waited. Christmas came early to the men of Bastogne. On December 22nd, supply planes flew through the flak to bring presents to the cheering troops on the ground. The presents came in Christmas colors – swinging prime red and green supply parachutes dropped desperately needed supplies that drifted across the gray sky down to the fields around the town. The bundles contained shells for the mute division artillery, gasoline for the vehicles, and food and ammunition for the troops.

The siege dragged on, but the tide had turned. The wreckage of enemy machines cluttered the roads and littered the slopes of the countryside. Aerial resupply had replenished the artillery and the guns of the 9th and 10th Armored Divisions. Meanwhile, to the South, hard hitting tanks of the 4th Armored Division were smashing their way north.

On the infrequent days of flying weather, the skies over Bastogne swarmed with P-47s circling and diving to strafe and bomb the concentration of enemy troops and armor. The front line was so undefined that American troops were frequently strafed and bombed. As the Germans had captured numerous American vehicles, it was difficult for the Air Corps to see where the enemy territory ended.

Enemy armor stabbed in vain at the stubbornly held line while artillery of all sizes pounded the frozen town. News spread of an imminent breakthrough by friendly armored elements to the South. At headquarters, commanders anxiously watched the arrow that marked the path of the 4th Armored Division as it pushed its way slowly north into heavy resistance. The critical period was over; the enemy encircling Bastogne had thrown everything into the assault and failed.

Relief came in the afternoon of December 26th, when the lead tanks of the 4th Armored Division contacted a roadblock on the southern perimeter. Almost too good to be true, troops of the roadblock kept the tank crew at gunpoint until they were sure, then shook hands. The exhausted, chilled rifleman merely said "Thank God."

Accompanying correspondents looked at the leveled buildings, the snow covered slopes littered with dead men and tanks, and the half frozen, battle-exhausted troops and named the besieged troops "The Battered Bastards of Bastogne."

General Maxwell D. Taylor came with the 4th Armored Division to take command of his beloved 101st Airborne Division, as he had been in Washington when his division was unexpectedly committed. Taylor had hopped the first overseas plane and arrived in Europe to impatiently sweat out the encirclement of Bastogne from the outside perimeter, while General McAuliffe was in command of the troops during his absence. After Bastogne, the rest of the war was anticlimactic for the 101st. The last fighting divisions of the German Army had been destroyed during the Battle of the Bulge.

In a pause during the battle, a civilian walks through one of the shelled out streets in Bastogne. *Courtesy National Archives.*

Surely this is a sign posted by some jokester, for there is no question nor doubt that these wrecked vehicles will not be impounded unless by a salvage crew after their destruction in Bastogne. *Courtesy National Archives.*

6

Germany

The charming, half-timber homes and comparative calm of the Alsace-Lorraine countryside was a welcome change after the vicious Bastogne campaign. For the first time in over a month, most of the troops were quartered indoors, and when the division finally settled into a defensive position in Haguenau, on the Moder River, many of the men on the line also had covered shelter. The Moder River ran through the center of Haguenau and the enemy held the Northeast bank. For 31 days the division held positions along the river. The days on the line were relatively quiet, except for extensive patrol activity by both the 101st and enemy forces, and occasionally the town came under heavy shelling. The days turned warmer and a welcome spring had arrived. By this time the division was relieved of duty in Haguenau and boarded 40X8 (40 men or 8 mules) trains for the base at Mourmelon-le-Grand.

A few days later, the airborne troops boarded trucks and headed towards the Rhine River. For most of the troops the war was already over – what lay ahead of them was more a wild chase down an infantryman's war. Recent battles had brought the Allied forces to the west bank of the Rhine on a broad front. An airborne operation was obviously in the cards, and the parachutists expected alert orders for the great jump across the Rhine. Large formations of C-46s crossed the skies over Mourmelon, and the men watched and wondered. Time passed slowly, but diversions like the Marlene Dietrich show, Mickey Rooney, and USO programs helped fill the days. Then one morning, vastly heavy-laden planes flew overhead. It was the 17th Airborne Division, and they were heading to drop zones over the Rhine. As the men of the 101st watched – from the ground for a change – they wished them luck and breathed a half sigh of relief. That was March 24th, and a few days later in early April the division boarded trucks and rode to the Ruhr. Their mission: to contain the western flank of the Ruhr pocket from the west bank of the Rhine.

Once again, the division occupied a line of static defense – this time in the ruined cities along the Rhine River across from the Ruhr pocket. Rich in industry, the towns of the Ruhr had undergone almost continual

In France once again, the division rested, trained, and was awarded the Presidential Unit Citation by General of the Army Dwight W. Eisenhower – the first time in the history of the American Army that an entire division was given the citation. That day was marked by a gala, brass-studded ceremony at Mourmelon. Previously this award was only given to units of regimental or smaller sizes, but the Citation was given to the 101st Division for its gallant defense of Bastogne. *Courtesy National Archives.*

bombing during the Allied attempts to knock out the German war machine. On April 12, 1945, in ceremonies throughout the division, men mourned the death of their President and Commander-in-Chief, Franklin D. Roosevelt.

In late April, the 101st moved from the Ruhr and started on a madcap chase that took them through southern Germany and into the Bavarian Alps and Austria.

7

The 1269th Engineer Combat Battalion

Willard White graduated from University of Louisiana's Engineering School, and was employed as an engineer with the Lower Colorado River Authority. In 1940 he married Lyndon B. Johnson's sister, Josefa Hermine Johnson. With the influence of the Johnson family, he joined the Army Reserves as an officer. Shortly after the sally attack by the Japanese at Pearl Harbor, on December 7, 1941, White was called to active duty. His early duties included the building of military roads and airfields in Alaska and Canada.

On March 30, 1944, White was reassigned to Camp Chaffee, Arkansas, and assigned the duty of organizing the 1269th Engineer Combat Battalion. The commander of Company A was Lt. Layton F. Jones, a veteran of the 1942/43 Japanese struggle for the Aleutian Islands. Jones had the reputation of being a great story teller, and always embellished the truth to strengthen the tale. One of the Platoon Sergeants was Robert Thibodaux, a handsome and aloof individual who was respected by those under his command. Every morning he appeared for duty in pressed fatigues, looking razor-sharp.

At Camp Chaffee they trained in bridge building, firing M-3 .45 caliber Grease Guns, bivouacking, and other training exercises. Seven months later, on October 18, 1944, the Battalion moved to Camp Kilmer, New Jersey.

They sailed unescorted from New York Harbor on board a converted luxury liner, the *SS Mariposa*. They sailed south, and on that first night off the Virginia coast the ship encountered a storm; the gale wind force blew waves that were 15 feet higher than the six-decked cruiser. That furious storm lasted three days.

Company A, 1269th Engineer was assigned the role of Military Police, complete with MP armbands. Their major duty was to keep the chow lines moving and maintain general order. Onboard the ship was a contingent of nurses. Lt. Layton Jones, Officer of the Guards, was called to the nurse's quarters, as Major Willard White was driving the nurses crazy. White had ignored the guard's order not to enter the nurse's quarters, and they were arguing with White to make him leave. Upon arriving, Jones ordered White to leave and had to threaten him with arrest.

White left in a huff. Jones later stated, "Imagine the trouble if he had raped any of those women. He was crazy about women."[1]

They entered the Mediterranean through the Strait of Gibraltar on November 4th, and after two days of smooth sailing along the coast of Spain the *SS Mariposa* docked at noontime in Marseilles, France. The battalion was assigned to the U.S. Seventh Army. They then marched to a staging area near Aix-en-Provence and spent three weeks in advanced demolition training while waiting for equipment and vehicles. During the training, Private Monaco was killed in an accident involving the premature explosion of three pounds of TNT.

On November 29th, the 1269th left Marseilles and traveled by motor convoy to Nice, France, where they were attached to the 44th AAA Brigade in support of the 442nd Regimental Combat Team, Japanese-American Niesi. For four months the members of the 1269th were engaged in operating water supply points, maintaining roads and bridges, painting signs, laying mine fields, and performing guard duty.

On January 1, 1945, Major Willard White was promoted to Lt. Col., along with the promotions of Captains Miles L. Wachendorf, Alton W. Bryant, and Lt. Ernst W. Childers. On February 11th, Staff Sergeant Richard W. Mills was killed in an accident when his ¼ ton truck tried to avoid a French truck at a point where the road was being repaired.

On March 23, 1945, the 1269th was assigned to the highly secretive Task Force (T-Force) of the Sixth Army Group. T-Force had been organized in the early stages of the war to recover German technology, such as patents and blueprints for heat-seeking missiles, jet aircraft, rockets, and other modern weapons of mass destruction. Members of T-Force wore blue helmets and could operate in any army or division's assigned area without prior approval. The battalion's primary responsibility was guard duty, the demolition of booby traps, and the laying of wire communication to T-Force Command Post.

But there was more to their role than this. The men of the 1269th daily lived with the rotten smell of death, occasional sniper fire, and always the looming threat of artillery. They could and did die in an instant. This realism occurred on April 3rd in Heidelberg. As Lt. Layton Jones and his driver were traveling down a secured street in Heidelberg, a shot rang out and his driver crumpled over the steering wheel. Jones took control of the jeep and brought it to a stop as the firing continued. The shots were coming from a third floor balcony. Several soldiers appeared, and Jones instructed them to fire back while he circled up behind the apartment and could see the shooter with a German army rifle and a pile of ammunition clips nearby. He banged the door open and jumped into the room as the shooter turned and took aim. Using his .45 caliber sidearm, Jones shot the person in the left shoulder and right breast. A thirteen-year old girl slid down the wall with blood coming out of her mouth, her last words, "You God damned American Pig."[2]

After this shocking confrontation, Jones decided he was through with the war and packed his bags and said he planned to walk to the Atlantic Ocean and go home. After several hours he was missed, and the commanding officer set out in a jeep to find Lt. Layton Jones. They found him dragging his bag down the road and had to force him into the jeep. Back in the company area he was sedated by the medics and sent to an Army General Hospital. Here he was treated for combat fatigue. He rejoined Company A, 1269th a month later in Munich.

The areas of operations during the remainder of April for the 1269th were Mannheim, Karlsruhe, Wurzburg, and Stuttgart. On April 12th, Lt. Warren C. Eckberg was assigned to Company A as a replacement. Eckberg was handsome, medium height, and youthful.

On April 30, 1945, the day Adolf Hitler committed suicide in his bunker at the Reich Chancellery in Berlin, the U.S. Seventh Army's XV Corps converged on Munich and cleared the city with ease. It is ironic that Hitler's death coincided with the capture of Munich, the birth and cradle of Nazism. The following day

T-Force, Sixth Army Group, entered the city. T-Force Command Post was headquartered in Munich in the Haus der Deutschen Kunst (German Art Museum). The modern building contained over one thousand paintings worth several thousand dollars each.

T-Force's high priority targets included the Führerbau and the Verwaltungsbau (Administrative Building). These four story marble twin buildings were Headquarters for the Nazi Party and located on the reconstructed Königplatz. To the rear of the Führerbau was an older building known as the Braunes Haus, the birthplace of the Nazi Party, and had been the original Nazi Party Headquarters until the Party grew too large to be housed in it. The complex was near the center of downtown Munich. The Braunes Haus had been destroyed above ground, but the other twin buildings were undamaged except for broken glass. These three large buildings were connected in a vast system of tunnels with underground kitchens, dining rooms, communications centers, and store rooms. Prior to the capture of Munich, on orders from the Reich Chancellery in Berlin, all documents in these buildings were to be evacuated or completely destroyed. Thus, over a period of eight days, eighty tons of documents were burned in the huge underground heating plant. Most of the documents not inflamed were loaded onto trucks and driven in the direction of Berchtesgaden.

In fact, after capture, this vast complex contained a large quantity of Nazi memorabilia and as described by an army captain, "so goddamn much you could never go through it unless you made it a definite target to exploit at great length."

T-Force definitely made this complex a target to profit by and removed tons of documents. The most important item removed was a row of steel cabinets alphabetically arranged, containing the complete files of all members of the Nazi Party. The finding of these Party records was a momentous bonanza for U.S. Military Intelligence and for indictments at the Nuremberg Trials. This Party file is in the U.S. National Archives today.

While T-Force was exploiting this target, American soldiers were taking action for their own shady deals. The 1269th Engineer Combat Battalion was in the fortunate position of acquiring some of the more prized items of World War II.

Their current assignment gave the men of the 1269th access to T-Force targets in Munich. Considerable looting had already taken place when the American forces took control of this building complex. Papers, junk, personal effects, photographs, and a large collection of miscellaneous items were scattered on the floors.

The underground of the three-building complex was crammed with valuable paintings, Party records, silverware, and many other valuable items gathered by the Nazi Party. Various units of the 45th Infantry Division and 163rd Engineer Combat Battalion guarded the buildings. During this time, PFCs Theodore J. Polski and John A. Fraser went to the Führerbau and noticed that several enlisted men, as well as officers from the 45th Infantry Division, were removing silverware for souvenirs. The guard did not seem to care, as two more captains, two colonels, and a Nurse Corps WAC captain joined the group, so Polski picked out a set of silverware with the initials A.H. and a Nazi swastika on each piece. Fraser himself collected eight sets of knives, forks, and spoons. During the excitement of removing this vast collection of silverware, Lieutenant Tigert noticed that soldiers from the 1269th loaded several trucks with large quantities of silverware.

Polski and Fraser returned to their Headquarters. Polski mailed his 80-piece set of silverware to his wife in St. Paul, Minnesota, and Fraser also mailed his booty home.

In the waterlogged basement of the Führerbau, an American Sergeant identified as "Sergeant Joseph" found a box that contained Hitler's most personal belongings, including his gold plated pistol. The box also contained Hitler's swastika ring; a tiny oil painted portrait of his mother; a framed photo of his dog, Blondi; and numerous pieces of silverware with the initials A.H. The most surprising find was the Swastika Blood Flag belonging to the unit of the Nazi

Party's greatest martyr, Horst Wessel, who fought in the Munich Putsch of 1923 and was murdered in 1930 by members of the Communist Party. Wessel composed the words and tune for the Horst Wessel song, which became the official song of the Nazi Party. The Sergeant's find turned up in the private collection of Ray Bily in 1981. The gold pistol, valued at more than a million dollars, was donated to the West Point Museum, where it is on display today. In addition to the soldiers, the Library of Congress would take possession of thousands of documents acquired from this Nazi Party complex by T-Force.

The lucrative looting of the Führerbau, the Verwaltungsbau, and the Braunes Haus continued unabated until the building complex was taken over by a Military Government Detachment. The Property Control Officer ordered the complex surrounded by barbed wire and guard stations. This put a stop to German civilians, American soldiers, and Displaced Persons climbing through windows and helping themselves to a wide array of valuable souvenirs.

The residence of Adolf Hitler (Prinzregenten Platz 16, Munich) was examined by T-Force and found to be occupied by the 45th Infantry Division, 179th Infantry Regiment, and some German civilians. The building was undamaged, and was only a few minutes walk from Eva Braun's house on Wasserburger Strasse 12.

Hans and Marie Schiffler lived in the basement of this building. She was the caretaker for the apartment building. Her husband was in the SA. Their son was a sergeant in the SS. She did not know the present location of her husband or son, or even if they were alive. Frau Schiffler further told T-Force that Hitler had last used the apartment about two years ago.

Else Gardner occupied the first floor on the right, and immediately told T-Force that she was British, due to a former marriage to a British citizen that had ended in divorce in 1934. Gardner's parents had occupied the apartment since 1915, and they had died recently. She showed the T-Force officer an occupying pass for the apartment dated June 6, 1942. Gardner said she last saw Hitler in the apartment complex on November 9, 1943. She concluded that Hitler was never in the building after that because he had not appeared in the air raid shelter during allied bombing raids. She also told the officer that Hitler had only infrequently occupied the apartment during the war years. The left apartment on the first floor was occupied by approximately 12 men assigned to military escort security duty.

The third floor, right apartment was Adolf Hitler's. Georg and Annie Winter occupied the left apartment. Georg served as the butler to Ritter von Epp, and his wife, Annie, was Hitler's confidential colleague and housekeeper. She was a member of Hitler's Munich inner circle. The couple had occupied the apartment since 1929. (In 1951 Annie Winter was arrested for trying to sell a suitcase full of Hitler's documents, which included his passport, gun permit, watercolor paintings, and photographs of his parents. The material is today in the Bavarian State Archives, Munich.)

It was in Hitler's apartment on the third floor that Hitler's niece, Angela (Geli) Raubal, killed herself. In 1930, Winifred Wagner (daughter-in-law of Richard) developed a close friendship with Hitler, and it was rumored that Hitler intended to marry her. Their intimacy resulted in several violent arguments between Hitler and his niece, Geli. Weary of these disputes and grieving over the death of her pet canary, she shot and killed herself with Hitler's revolver on September 17, 1931. It is most likely that their relationship was platonic, but he did adore her. Her room was preserved as a shrine. Frau Annie Winter sealed off the room at Hitler's orders and opened it only on the anniversary of Geli's birth and death. Hitler never once entered the room. A T-Force officer stated "There was an eeriness in the room. The shade on the only window was drawn and her clothes and cosmetics were just as she had left them."

From Hitler's apartment T-Force removed the following:

Dienstalterliste der SS as of October 1, 1934.
Strength reports of the SS, July 1935.
Six volumes *Mein Kampf*, 1927 edition, second volume.
Three volumes *Mein Kampf*, 1929 edition, second volume.
One Volume *Mein Kampf*, Volkesusgabe, 1930 edition.
Report of Iran by Kusenpolitisches amt der NSDAP.
One Copy Eviler(?) *LuftschutzmAufbau und Schulung*.
Illustrated Volume *Die Führer des Reichsheeres*.
Twelve photo albums with early pictures of Hitler and friends.
Collection of Photographs "Der ewige Jude".
Historical photographs of Party celebrations, Party offices,
    and Personalities and world events
Collection of rare books manuscripts,
    photo albums dedicated to Hitler.
Miscellaneous letters addressed to Mrs. Annie Winter and
    photographs believed to be Georg Winter.
Confidential report to the Reichsleitung of the NSDAP,
    September 1924.
Article dedicated to Hitler's "Ein officieles Britisches Ringestänänis
Five school magazines of Hitler's school in Linz.
Ortzschaftenverseichnis für den Freistaat Bayern.
List of German telephone nets to foreign countries.
One volume commemorating Mussolini's visit to Munich.
One original letter by Ulrich von Hütten dedicated to Hitler.
Two rare volumes of the Holy Script
Collection of historical slides

Not removed was Hitler's library, containing many books on architecture and the history of World War I, scrolls, and other items dedicated to Hitler. Two safes were opened by combat engineers attached to T-Force in the presence of officers of the 45th Infantry Division, 179th Infantry Regiment. The safe contained Hitler's personal stationery, silver picture frames, a stained glass window, silverware, paintings, cigarette case, bronze medals, copies of *Mein Kampf*, and other books. These items were left in the care of the 179th. Many of these items found their way into the pockets of the members of the 45th Infantry Division. From Hitler's apartment, their museum in Oklahoma City has several copies of *Mein Kampf* and also copies of the book in foreign languages.

Upon completion of the initial phase of the Munich operation, the Battalion Commander of the 1269th Engineer Combat Battalion was commended by the Commander of Sixth Army Group T-Force for the success of the initial operation and for the speed with which the early targets were exploited.

During his tour in Munich, Lt. Col. Willard White managed to obtain several heavily decorated, souvenir beer steins from the Hofbrauhaus, Hitler's base for his 1923 unsuccessful putsch. Also here he looted the demitasse cups, silver decanters, and goblets signifying an alliance between France and Italy.

Berchtesgaden was an offshoot of the Munich operation, and on May 5, 1945, the Second Platoon of Company A, along with Lt. Col. Willard White, was sent to Berchtesgaden to exploit targets in that area. And White did exploit Berchtesgaden. From Adolf Hitler's mountain retreat (the Berghof), White took over a 100 pieces of flat silverware and dozens of tea pots, coffee pots, cream and sugar bowls, gravy dishes, trays, covered dishes, salt and pepper shakers, napkins, towels, and personal stationary. Every piece was distinguished by the Third Reich German Eagle surmounting a swastika and the initials A.H. The silver was all marked "800," denoting silver.

From Hermann Göring's own bed, White took an enormous white wool blanket. "Its fine quality again proves that nothing was too good for the Nazis."

Lt. Col. Willard White also looted dozens of Dresden figurines, delicate porcelain figures from France, whole collections of German officers' swords and dueling pieces, and a heavy SS dagger handsome in design and inscribed with the storm trooper's name and date (1938), along with the SS motto marked in the blade. While fighting through southwest France, White had taken crystal goblets from the palace of Louis Napoleon III. This entire collection he mailed to his wife, Josefa White, at 1900 Townes Lane, Austin, Texas, his home.

White wrote, "That as a matter of fact, he was looking upon the ruins [Obersalzberg] when he learned the war was over." This was May 8, 1945, and two days later Company A, 2nd Platoon would chisel their way through cement into Reichsmarschall Herman Göring's treasure hidden in Aladdin's Cave at Berchtesgaden.

8
The Capture of Berchtesgaden

The German redoubt was a serious consideration for the Allies, as intelligence information indicated that a large buildup of German troops was taking place in the Bavarian and Austrian Alps. Hitler had issued orders in March 1945 for this area to be heavily fortified. Thus, 14,000 freight cars of food and ammunition poured through the Munich marshalling yard, creating one large traffic jam of trains. Thousands of laborers had worked day and night for a month building fortifications. The center of the redoubt was to be Hitler's vacation retreat near Berchtesgaden. In the basement was a very advanced communication system that could be used to coordinate a long struggle in this mountainous area. The defense was to be a ring of steel around Berchtesgaden. Allied forces were apprehensive that thousands of die-hard Nazis would fight a protracted war from these fortifications. The plans went astray with Hitler's decision to personally stay in Berlin and defend the city from the mighty Soviet Army. These ill-advised tactics were finished when Hitler committed suicide by firing a bullet through his head.

As the American Seventh Army advanced past Munich, it was obvious the German Army was beaten and demoralized by the obvious defeat, as they surrendered in large masses or continued in a disorganized retreat barely ahead of the Allied Army. The highways were jammed with a weird conglomeration of humanity, Allied soldiers, captured transportation, and liberated slave workers on foot and horseback headed for France, Belgium, and Holland, as well as countries in Eastern Europe. Long columns of German soldiers, too many to be guarded, were seen marching towards POW collection points in the rear areas. It would have taken an entire division alone to guard the vast hordes of enemy soldiers that surrendered during those last days of the war. Instead, enemy officers were put in charge and told to march their men to the rear. High-ranking politicians and military figures of the Nazi regime were taken by the 101st Division. Among them were Robert Ley, Julius Streicher, and Generals Albert Kesselring and Gottlieb Berger.

Another person of interest "captured" was Adolf Hitler's sister, Paula, who was living in Berchtesgaden in the home of Dietrich Eckart, the Führer's favorite Nazi poet. Paula was interrogated by CIC agent George Allen. She told the agent she had bought a little house in Weiten, Austria, with the help of her brother. In April 1945, as the massive Red Army advanced, Hitler had sent a car for her and she traveled to Berchtesgaden, where she was housed in the luxurious Berchtesgadener Hof. With the advance of the U.S. Seventh Army she moved in with Eckart. Paula further stated:

> I liked my brother Adolf best of all, in spite of our differences in age [7 years]. My relations with him were always good, and as I was not ambitious, I never appeared at public festivals with him. I do not believe my brother ordered the crimes committed to innumerable human beings in the concentration camps or that he ever knew of these crimes. He was still my brother, no matter what happened.

At this point Paula broke into tears and the interrogation ended.[1]

Soldiers of the 101st Airborne Division advance up the steep mountainous road from Berchtesgaden to Hitler's retreat at Obersalzberg. *Courtesy the Pratt Museum, U.S. Army.*

The chalet of Adolf Hitler. Initially called Haus Wachenfeld, it was renamed the Berghof and was a large double-decked building with a wide terrace, an underground garage, and large bomb shelter. *Courtesy of Pratt Museum, U.S. Army.*

An early morning May snow shrouds the blackened bomb damage after the April 25, 1945, bombing by 350 British Lancaster planes of Hitler's Berghof and surrounding buildings on the Obersalzberg. *Courtesy the Pratt Museum, U.S. Army.*

A paratrooper of the 326th Airborne Engineer Battalion uses a heavy bulldozer to clear snow and rubble from the road leading to Hitler's Eagle's Nest. *Courtesy the Pratt Museum, U.S. Army.*

Hermann Göring's Obersalzberg summer home, before and after the Allied bombing. (top) *Courtesy Library of Congress*, (bottom) *Courtesy National Archives*.

Additional bomb damage on the Obersalzberg location of the summer homes for several Third Reich leaders. *Courtesy the Pratt Museum, U.S. Army*.

9

The Payoff

The 3rd Infantry Division had landed in North Africa in November 1942. During the invasion of Italy, the 3rd landed at Salerno and fought several furious battles in the mountains, and later assaulted Anzio. The Division landed at the Bay of Cavalarie, France, on August 15, 1944, for a drive through southern France into Germany. All this fighting with very little publicity, although Medal of Honor winner Audie Murphy, the most decorated soldier of World War II, was a member of this division.

After the battle for Munich, the division's next objective was Salzburg, Austria. The autobahn bridge to Salzburg had been destroyed, and the 3rd Division located a damaged railroad bridge a mile south of the autobahn at Piding, Germany. There was also a small wooden bridge in close proximity, both crossing the Saalach River. After crossing the Saalach, the 3rd Division took Piding on May 4th without any opposition. The 3rd Division's 7th Regiment still controlled both these bridges about five miles southwest of Salzburg. To get to Berchtesgaden, which was 14 miles away, a person would have to use one of these bridges. The Division Commander, Gen. John W. O'Daniel, realized he held the key to the last remaining prized possession of what was left of the Greater Reich; the prestige of capturing the homes of the highest-ranking Nazi leaders, along with their most treasured possessions. What an opportunity to loot!

That morning, O'Daniel discussed with Colonel John A. Heintges the possibility of taking Berchtesgaden. Without hesitation Heintges ordered the 1st and 3rd Battalions to move out. The troops, along with armor and artillery, crossed the railroad trestle, as one battalion went through Bad Reichenhall, while the other continued south down the autobahn. They were to meet in Berchtesgaden. O'Daniel then gave the order that no one could use the bridges. Therefore, the bridges remained closed to the French 2nd Armored Division and the 101st Airborne; both units had orders to take Berchtesgaden. French General Jacques Leclerc made a feeble attempt to cross the bridge but was denied access.

Soldiers of the 3rd Infantry Division enjoy a bottle of wine at Hitler's Eagle's Nest atop Kehlstein Mountain. The soldiers captured Berchtesgaden on May 4, 1945. The 101st Airborne entered a day later and were given credit for the capture of Berchtesgaden. This recognition gained a life of its own, and even historian Stephen E. Ambrose, in his book *Band of Brothers*, reports this unintended error as fact. *Courtesy National Archives.*

Members of the French 2nd Armored Division lost little time in looting, as one member carries a trunk full of Cognac and Champaign taken from Hitler's Berghof. His buddy, wearing the cook's hat, has a large bag slung over his shoulder, while the soldier following them is cradling trophies in both arms. *Courtesy National Archives.*

At 4:00 in the afternoon on May 4, 1945, the 3rd Infantry Division added another feather to its well-plumed hat and captured Berchtesgaden, the site of Hitler's summer home and his famous Eagles Nest. The halftracks and jeeps mounted with 50 caliber machine guns took up positions in the city square as German District Official Emil Jacob drove down from his mountain retreat and surrendered the town to members of the 3rd Infantry Division. The streets were lined with German officers in their long grey coats, awaiting orders from the German command that would never come. They quickly surrendered along with Hermann Göring's nephew Fritz. Then the 3rd Infantry radioed back that they had taken Berchtesgaden, and the bridge across the Saalach River was opened as the French 2nd Armored Division crossed, followed by elements of the 101st.

Members of the 1st and 3rd battalion began exploiting the town. Lt. Sherman Pratt took his platoon and some tanks to the Obersalzberg, Hitler's summer retreat, now in ruins because of being saturated by bombs by the Royal Air Force on a clear spring morning on April 25, 1945. The soldiers did some minor looting and could not believe the shelves stocked with wine, hams, cheese, and cans containing pickles. The remaining troops were down in Berchtesgaden, availing themselves to warehouses full of whiskey, cheese, and other foods. They quickly loaded six trucks with Johnny Walker's Red Label, Black Label, and American whiskey and sent the trucks to Division Headquarters, Salzburg, Austria.

May 8, 1945: after three years, 152 days, and 125,670 Christian crosses and Stars of David on graves in 54 cemeteries in Europe, the war was over for U.S. forces in Europe. *Courtesy the Pratt Museum, U.S. Army*.

Around 8:00 P.M. the first troops of the French 2nd Armored Division, under the command of General Leclerc, reached Berchtesgaden from the Bad Reichenhall Road. The French troops, steeped in looting, immediately blocked off the ends of the main streets with halftracks to prevent anyone from leaving and went through the houses and shops, throwing valuables out the doors and windows. What they decided to keep they loaded aboard the halftracks and then left. On May 5th, a Saturday morning, Colonel Heintges and a French staff officer worked out the occupation zone by dividing the town along the railroad track that ran through the middle of Berchtesgaden. This would be a short-lived agreement.

That same May 5th, in the afternoon, the 506th Regiment of the 101st Airborne Division entered Berchtesgaden. Entering the town had not been a cakewalk for the 101st, as Pvt. Nick Kozovosky and PFC Claude E. Ranking were the last two combat causalities of the Division. That same day, Colonel Heintges led some of the soldiers of 7th Regiment, 3rd Division up to Obersalzberg. They were accompanied by more than a hundred news journalists. They were stopped by a French roadblock and finally received permission to continue after Heintges proposed a joint flag raising. After a brief ceremony the Americans left. The next day, to their surprise, 3rd Division was ordered back to Salzburg, their original objective.

The French tankers continued to loot and riddle the town with bullets. A drunken French soldier shot to death Georg Gethlein, head of the construction workers, outside the Platterhof Hotel. There was a lot of "bad talk" between the American and French soldiers, and as a result, on May 6th, the French were ordered to leave Berchtesgaden. They machine gunned Göring's train in Unterstein, continued looting, and moved on to Innsbruck.

Again on May 5th, Franz Brandenburg, the personal bodyguard of Emmy Göring, arrived at Unterstein, and a startling sight awaited him. It seemed that the complete population was at the small train station, fighting their way into the freight cars, carrying heavy loads of booty, cutting up large carpets, and beating and scratching each other in their greed to conquer a part of Göring's "heritage." Also at the station were several freight cars containing Göring's valuable collection of liquor, which had arrived four weeks earlier. As the locals raided the liquor, their drunkenness added to the chaos. When questioned later about this brazen looting, several would admit that they were too drunk to remember what happened.

At the scene several women cut an eighteenth century French Aubusson rug into four pieces. It was still so large that several of the women, namely Fraus Ostermeister, Beer, and Winkler subdivided one of the quarters into three separate pieces. Bertha Weigert took 82 pieces of silverware, two candlesticks, and four glasses. Herr Hinterbrandtner carried off a valuable old Persian rug. Else Schuler grabbed a silver box with precious stones, a silver fish plate, and a nutcracker. Berta Meigert took several knives, spoons, and Bohemian glasses. Three of the glasses had Göring's coat of arms engraved onto them. Frau Pfnürl took a small triptych painting. Herr Scharper borrowed a small hand-pulled wagon from his neighbor Klara Eder and carted it away loaded with loot. Count Hudicek took several paintings, a silver mug, and other valuables. Gottfried Volpe swiped a Miro painting that Göring had purchased from Holland.

Thus paintings, rugs, gold coins, and other valuables, as well as sugar, cigarettes, coffee, and expensive liquors found their way into the homes of the people of Unterstein. These valuables were hidden in homes, barns, woodsheds, haystacks, and even under manure piles.

Franz Brandenburg saw more than a dozen valuable paintings lying on the ground near the station. Trying to take control of the mob, he began to give out Schnapps and soap. This calmed the crowd for about 30 minutes as he collected the paintings and put them back into the freight cars. Shortly thereafter, Oberkommisär Boos, the local policeman, arrived and reluctantly fired a shot into the air; as a result most of the looters scattered and disappeared. Later, at 4:30 p.m., the Allied Troops arrived in Unterstein, disarmed Boos, and ordered him and two older men to collect the objects strewn about the train and the immediate area of the train station. It took the three Germans until 2:00 the following morning to pick up and store the items.

After the battle of Berchtesgaden, the steep, winding road that led high up to what had been Hitler's mountain retreat above Berchtesgaden was heavy with traffic. American soldiers and French troops in jeeps, trucks, swanky captured limousines, and on foot were going to and from the Berghof and the vast expanse of buildings and grounds that surrounded it.

The Americans and French were now staging a celebration on the rubble grounds and buildings Hitler had built. There was a lot to celebrate with, for the wine cellars of the Berghof and especially the cellar of the great guest house contained thousands of bottles of fine French wines, cognac, champagne, and Rhine wines. In the store rooms of the guest house were enough dishes, silverware, and frozen and canned goods to last for years. One of the servants said the food could last for 10 years, or "until the war had been decided." But the war had been decided ahead of schedule and the wine, food, silverware, and countless other items were disappearing with amazing speed. During the looting Mrs. Ellen Bluethgen, a cook still at Obersalzberg, was asked if it was true that the Führer chewed on rugs when he became excited. She flushed angrily and replied, "Only you Americans believe such nonsense."[1]

The scene at Berchtesgaden was one of bedlam. The stream of trucks, jeeps, and limousines lengthened. Moroccans in red fezzes carried away enormous portraits that they were almost certain to toss away in a short time. Americans on foot carried bottles which they were almost certain to drink in a short time; in fact, there were many who had already drunk heavily of the Führer's hospitality, for all along the ground were strewn empty bottles that had once held Burgundy, Moselle, champagne, and other fine wines.

Most of the buildings were gutted beyond recognition. The guest house where Benito Mussolini once lived had been hit directly by a bomb. The home of Martin Bormann, national organizer of the Nazi party, was smashed to rubble. Hermann Göring's home on a small hill above the Berghof seemed to sway in the wind, an empty house except for an enormous bathtub which had been flown from Berlin two years previously. When the Americans arrived some of the ruins still smoked from fires started by British bombing attacks. Also smoking were the heavy green camouflage nets over most of the buildings. Hundreds of tall slender pines that thickly wooded the estate lay broken like matchsticks from the bomb concussions. Sections of the woods were stripped bare from direct hits. Tiny waterfalls from the hills rippled over the debris of paper, books, bricks, stone, and empty wine bottles. "It looks to me," said an American infantry colonel, "like they were expecting to defend this place with wine bottles."[2]

The following day the 101st received a message that all troops were to stand fast in their present position, as the enemy Army Group G had surrendered. Two days later, May 8th, all German forces surrendered. On that same day the 506th Regiment was ordered to move 15 miles south to the resort town of Zell am See. Replacing the 506th was Headquarters 101st Airborne Division, the 327th Glider Infantry Regiment, and the 501st Airborne Regiment coming up from Mourmelon, France. Therefore, the 101st stayed, and the unit that seized Berchtesgaden was quickly forgotten by history, as the 101st was credited with the capture of Berchtesgaden. After all, the 101st was debatably the most famous division in the U.S. Army.

The Berchtesgaden region was quite removed from the ravaged battlefield and destroyed cities of Europe. Except for Obersalzberg, the homes were intact and the public services were fully functional. The whole area resembled a Bavarian picture postcard. But Berchtesgaden was not the target of all this frenzied military activity; Obersalzberg, two miles west and Hitler's mountain retreat, was the prized possession. In 1924, after he had finished his prison term, Hitler rented a small chalet on the northern slope of Obersalzberg Mountain in the Bavarian Alps. The white stucco brown stained chalet built prior to World War I was called Haus Wachenfeld, and was two thousand feet above sea level. When Hitler became Chancellor in 1933, he ordered an extensive enlargement of his mountain retreat. The indefatigable Martin Bormann was placed in charge of the remodeling and immediately evicted the long established inhabitants of 18 farms, 35 private homes, several hotels, and a children's sanatorium. The project included a "summer" Reichskanzlei (State Chancellery) at Stangass (a suburb of Berchtesgaden), a large security system with SS guards, and also a new modern train station in Berchtesgaden. The project, using a labor force of 6,000 men, took five years.

The Summer Reichskanzlei was occupied as the Command Post of the 101st Airborne Division. *Courtesy the Pratt Museum, U.S. Army.*

The Berghof, as Hitler renamed the remolded Haus Wachenfeld, was a large white double-decked bungalow with a wide terrace, a garage cut into the side of the mountain, and a nice, large, deep bomb shelter with complete housekeeping facilities. Most of the first floor of the Berghof was taken up by the Great Hall that was on two levels connected by a flight of steps with a number of cozy nooks. Tapestries ornamented the walls, two huge chandeliers provided light, and the floor was covered with carpeting over which were scattered Oriental rugs.

Hitler's study, which he liked to call his workroom, was on the second floor next to his living quarters, and was a large room with two full-length windows and a glass-front bookshelf. The guest rooms were furnished in ornate, heavy, eighteenth century German fashion lightened by framed watercolor paintings done by Hitler himself. The large terrace with wooden tables and chairs sheltered by striped awnings was the most blissful and fashionable place at the Berghof, and here all the visitors flocked, as smoking was allowed on the large terrace but not in the Berghof, and smoking was definitely in vogue during this era. It was here in the Berghof, in 1938, that Benito Mussolini, Neville Chamberlin, and Edouard Daladier signed the peace treaty that set the stage for World War II.

Impressive as the Berghof was, it paled in comparison to the Adlerhorst (Eagle's Nest) built at the top of neighboring Mount Kehlstein. It took three thousand workmen three years to build the Adlerhorst and the road leading up the mountainside almost to it. The Adlerhorst, completed in 1938, consisted of a living room with a large fireplace, expensive furniture, and several windows from which there was an exceptionally great view. In addition, there was a large dining room that seated about 30 people, a breakfast room, bedrooms, and a kitchen.

Like the Third Reich, which was built to last a thousand years, Hitler's Obersalzberg was now a heap of rubbish mostly destroyed by the Royal Air Force bombing of April 25, 1945. It is doubtful that the large iron barrels located around the Obersalzberg were used to hide the valley during this Allied bombing. These barrels, which were under great pressure, released a white chemical that rapidly turned into clouds of fog. The chemical fog burned nearby grass and charred the trees. The Berghof had only been slightly damaged by the bombing raid, but on May 5th, when it became obvious that the Allies were going to take Obersalzberg, SS troops set fire to the building, destroying all the fittings in the main entrance hall except some squat red marble pillars. Hitler's study, with its famous large windows, was charred and empty, with only the frame, and at the opposite side was a large, wrought-iron fireplace decorated with figures of three German soldiers. The staircase was in fairly good condition, but most of the Berghof was destroyed, all except for the basement. Searched by T-Force, the residence contained a large film library, movie projector, architectural drawings, and the living quarters of Eva Braun, Hitler's mistress. There were two entrances to an air raid shelter behind the building and two towards the valley on the other side of the road. This tunnel connected Bormann tunnel, and it contained living quarters, an operation room, dentist office, phonograph record collection, library, and food supplies.

At the time of the bombing, Göring was under arrest by the SS at his Berchtesgaden home, which was destroyed by the bombing. He and his family survived the attack, as they were in the tunnel complex next to his home. The next day, Göring was taken by the SS to his Mauterndorf Castle. Martin Bormann's home was almost completely destroyed. There was an entrance in the basement that connected with the Vorder Eck (the large tunnel complex that averaged 100 feet in depth at Obersalzberg) and tunnel connection to the Berghof tunnels. The Bormann tunnel contained food supplies, living quarters, an air raid warning center, and the former command post of an anti-aircraft flack battalion.

During this chaotic time (May 2nd), the SS guards abandoned their post, leaving the gates swingy freely at Obersalzberg. It did not take the local population long to walk up the well paved road into the complex of the bombed houses of Albert Spears, Martin Bormann, Hermann Göring, Joseph Goebbels, and of course Adolf Hitler. The kindergarten nursery for the children of the Nazi elite was undamaged. The locals were dismayed at the exaggerated lifestyle of the Nazi elite, while they had severe rationing for years. The first items taken by the hungry populace were rice, beans, lentils, flour, sugar, butter, and oats, followed by clothes, shoes, and soap. The good citizens of Berchtesgaden then took everything they could move: paintings, silver, china, and books. What restricted their looting was the lack of large trucks, as wheelbarrows, push carts, laundry baskets, and hay wagons pulled by oxen were used in carrying the ill-gotten gains down the one small mountain road. Max Brandner, owner of the bread and breakfast Haus Erika, looted Hitler's large collection of silverware from the Berghof.

The Gutshof, a barn-like building complex just below the destroyed Nazi homes, was constructed as a model for future farms of the Nazi empire. It was almost undamaged and contained large two story high wooden barrels of wine and cider that was carried away by the local Germans in milk cans. These connecting tunnels were in the construction stage and led to the vicinity of Gästehaus Hoher Göll, undamaged, that now served as the Headquarters of T-Force, Sixth Army Group, XXI Corps. The building had been the office of Martin Bormann and contained many teletype machines. The tunnel below Gästehaus Hoher Göll contained large generators that could supply electricity for all of the underground passages.

Great quantities of ammunition, weapons, and demolitions were found in most of the tunnels. The Hitler/Bormann tunnel was designed in such a manner that each passage could be defended by built-in machine guns. T-Force removed several telephone directories, drawings of a portion of Vorder Eck, codes of wireless radio stations, reports of commercial relations between Germany and Italy, and a manuscript (Cross-sectional view of the tasks of the German Cultural Center). A thorough search of the underground tunnels conducted by T-Force yielded no documents of importance. T-Force arrested Mr. Noris of the large construction firm Arge Holzmann, Held, and Francke, who was in charge of the construction work on the tunnels and local bunkers. Noris claimed no knowledge of the purpose of the tunnels and stated emphatically that to his knowledge no documents were hidden in the labyrinth complex.

The snow at the entrance of the elevator to the Eagle's Nest has melted, and it is now guarded by a member of the 101st Airborne. *Courtesy National Archives.*

The Eagle's Nest, located on the top of Mount Kehlstein, overlooked the entire Berchtesgaden/Königsee area. A paved road led from the Berghof to the base of a steep cliff on which the Eagle's Nest had been constructed. When captured by Allied forces, about one half of the road was covered with snow and there was the constant threat of an avalanche. The road passed through several tunnels constructed just to reach the entrance to the Eagle's Nest. At the end of the road was a large underground entrance covered with snow that contained an elevator that led directly to the top. The elevator was not working, and the house could only be reached by a steep side trail. When viewed by T-Force, a small amount of canned food and a large supply of carbonated water were found in the basement, but most of the food, silverware, and other articles of souvenir value had been removed by previous visitors.

The large, three-story Platterhof Hotel, with 350 rooms and hot and cold running water, was well preserved, and contained several restaurants and recreation rooms. This was because early in the war the hotel was used for recovering wounded German officers. At the time of the arrival of the 101st, the Platterhof Hotel was overflowing with German military causalities. These officers were reassigned to other medical facilities, and now the 101st Airborne Division occupied the low-ceiling, cell-like hotel, each room with pine beds and a desk lamp. Most of the furnishings had been destroyed by the French 2nd Armored Division. They smashed most of the windows and marched off with the china, glassware, wall decorations, and the hotel's plentiful stocks of wine.

German civilians had initiated the looting, and when the American and French forces took over, the looting continued for several more days. Memento hunters were in their heaven, with souvenirs from the homes of the high-ranking Nazis. The mailbags were soon stuffed with treasures that they mailed home. The cellars of the beautiful alpine villages were loaded to street level with wines and liquors that had been acquired from the conquered countries of Europe. It was indeed a paradise for the airborne soldier.

Berchtesgaden was flush with paratroopers, and the units of the 101st Division occupied several villages a few miles across the German border in the Austrian Alps. Many of the towns were fashionable resorts, and men of the division swam, fished, hunted, climbed mountains, and lived in comparative luxury in fashionable hotels and homes formerly occupied by members of the Nazi Party.

Arriving from Munich on May 8, 1945, were Lt. James J. Rorimer and Lt. Calvin Hathaway, Monuments, Fine Art and Archival Officers of the Seventh Army who had traveled to Berchtesgaden. They were looking for the bulk of the Reichsmarschall's art collection. At Obersalzberg the men scrambled over piles of rubble and burned furnishings, a result of the devastation bombing by the Royal Air Force. The underground passageways, complete with air-conditioned living quarters, had withstood the bombing raid. The two men made a thorough search of the houses of Hitler, Göring, and Martin Bormann. They were not alone, as the follow-up echelons of French and American soldiers were wholesale looting, and there was a mad scramble to liberate everything movable. Rorimer noticed that there were hundreds of thousands of feet of Nazi motion picture film unrolled and scattered all over the mountain top. They traveled through the endless passageways connecting the homes.

The two officers determined that the only works of art remaining in Göring's bombed-out chalet were unimportant decorative pieces. The previous Christmas, as he left Obersalzberg, Göring had ordered that all the fine art in his home be placed in the secure tunnel next to his home to be safe from Allied bombing. At the entrance of one of the tunnels next to Göring's home was a glazed terra cotta tondos, a great example of Della Robbia work. It had been abandoned by looters because of the heavy weight. Rorimer pointed out the then-undamaged Della Robbia and insisted the valuable sculpture be safeguarded. The Della Robbia remained there for three weeks and was run over by a truck. It was only upon

The above sixteenth century sculpture by Luca Della Robbia, *Bust of a Man with a Fruit Wreath*, was discarded on the road by a looter that found it too heavy to carry. The bust was acquired for Göring from the Mannheimer Collection. After it was partially destroyed by a vehicle the remnants were in some measure restored (right). The bust was returned to Holland on December 2, 1946, by the U.S. Army. *Both photos Courtesy National Archives.*

his return, a week later, that the sculpture was retrieved by Rorimer. That day, May 8, 1945, Rorimer and Hathaway returned to Munich without a clue as to the location of the cache of Göring's art collection.

In droves the press, high-ranking generals, and American congressmen arrived to see the ruins of Hitler's home and the Eagle's Nest. All these visitors seeing the presence of so many members of the 101st Airborne makes it easy to realize how they were credited with being first in Berchtesgaden, as it became an accepted fact. The influx of Allied visitors averaged 3,000 a day, with that figure reaching 10,000 on a weekend. Then reigning Congressman Lyndon B. Johnson arrived to view the attraction and visit with his brother-in-law, Willard White. He admired one of White's German Lugers and asked White for one of the pistols. White's response was a bit harsh, as he told Johnson to get one the same way he did – off a dead German soldier.

Arriving with Divisional Headquarters and Headquarters was Major Robert Smith and Captain Harry Anderson of the Division's Military Government Section, G-5. The 43-year-old Smith had joined the army on May 7, 1942, and, like many older professional men, the lawyer was assigned to Military Government. After several assignments in the U.S., he attended the School of Military Government at the University of Virginia and was assigned to the 101st Airborne Division on December 3, 1944.

Harry V. Anderson (0923580), born March 22, 1902, joined the army on March 27, 1943. A successful businessman, Anderson had founded the highly successful *Interior Design* magazine in 1932, shortly after his marriage. His family life was a dismal failure that ended in a divorce in the mid-'30s, with Anderson marrying for the second time in 1936. His military duties had paralleled

The 42-year old Capt. Harry V. Anderson, from Ossining, NY, was a husky fellow with red hair and a boyish manner. *Courtesy National Archives.*

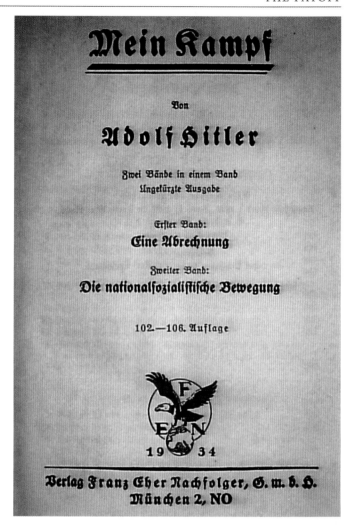

The most common item looted during World War II were books from Hitler's private library. The single title most looted would be his tome *Mein Kampf* (My Struggle). The book with a torn jacket cover is on the left, with the title page on the right identifying the book as published in 1934.

Smith's, and while reporting to Smith, Anderson would be placed in charge of collecting and safeguarding the Göring treasure in Berchtesgaden.

Sergeant Richard P. Jeffrey, Jr., Army Air Corps, while touring Berchtesgaden, took the above *Mein Kampf* and ten more books from Adolf Hitler's library. One of the books titled *Angriff*, authored by Joseph Goebbels, contains on the flyleaf a one-line written inscription addressed to "My Führer" and was signed by Dr. Goebbels, dated December ??, 1935. The inscription reads "Meine Führer in admiration and gratitude Dr. Goebbels." These books are today in a private collection.

Most of the books that constitute the Hitler library were discovered in a salt mine near Berchtesgaden haphazardly stashed in schnapps crates with the Reich Chancellery address on them. They were uncovered by soldiers of the 101st Airborne Division. After a lengthy initial evaluation at the U.S. Munich Central Collection Point, the books, numbering 3,000, were shipped to the United States and transferred in January 1952 to the Library of Congress.

10

Aladdin's Cave

A large building was used as a headquarters for the Luftwaffe in the Berchtesgaden area. It was located in the southern part of the town, off the road leading to Unterstein. A three story bunker system 60 feet deep and a quarter of a mile long was built into the hill beneath the headquarters building, where the bulk of Hermann Göring's art collection was discovered by American troops in May 1945. This large bomb-proof bunker appeared empty when first examined by U.S. forces. The treasure had been concealed in the lower level, hidden by a freshly poured concrete wall. After discovery, the bunker would always be known as Aladdin's Cave.

Headquarters 101st Airborne Division
Military Government Office
APO 472, U.S. Army
14 June 1945
5. Discoveries: The greater portion of the art treasures located in the Division's area had been discovered on May 11, and the work of removing them to place of safety, cataloguing and preserving them from further damage had already begun. The contents of Göring's tunnels at his summer home and on his private train abandoned in Berchtesgaden constituted the greater part of this art.

This above paragraph is the only official document that the authors could find regarding the bulk of Hermann Göring's art treasure concealed in Aladdin's Cave. The discovery of the cave begins with two different versions, but both have the same ending.

The first version is Lt. Layton Jones, Commander, Company A, 1269th Engineer Combat Battalion, reportedly initiated a conversation with a German engineer who claimed to have been responsible for constructing a large bunker under the south end of Göring's hunting lodge property in Berchtesgaden. As they entered the large bunker, the engineer stated that when they built the bunker a large room was right at the bottom third level. Jones noticed that fresh concrete appeared to cover the entrance to a potential side room. Using "certain sounding techniques" they located a place

Gregor Erhardt's *Belle Allemande* from the Louvre The most outstanding piece of sculpture acquired by the Reichsmarschall was this life size nude, lime wood statue of Magdalene. Erhardt carved this masterpiece about 1510, and it decorated a church in Augsburg for centuries and was offered for sale on the German art market and purchased by the Louvre in 1902. This was the first piece of art work noticed by Captain Harry Anderson and recovered from Aladdin's Cave. He was infatuated with this sculpture and took several personal photographs of the statue. While being transported to Berchtesgaden two fingers were broken. *Courtesy National Archives*

in the concrete wall that sounded as though there was a hollow space at that point. Jones sent word back to the platoon to have the troops bring their picks and shovels. It is logical that Jones would have met an engineer, as T-Force had apprehended the engineers responsible for construction of the Obersalzberg bunkers and were interrogating them at this time. The official word was that the location was obtained by U.S. Army Intelligence from a prisoner of war, and this is in line with that statement.

The second version is that in an undated, unsigned letter to Agnes Mongan, Harry Anderson had written that one day a German engineer came to the 101st headquarters with information that he had built a cider mill for Hitler. Anderson left with the engineer to find the cider mill, reasoning that the paratroopers had had enough cognac and could use a change in their drinking habits.

A few days later, the engineer flagged down Anderson's jeep. Anderson asked the engineer if he had helped build the large bunker the previous year. He told Anderson that indeed he had, and would show him the large cement bunker. Anderson responded that the lights were off, as they were throughout the region, but the enterprising engineer produced some flashlights and they walked through the large cavern. At one point the German engineer pointed to a wall and said if he was not mistaken there should be a door where there was now fresh cement.

Lieutenant Layton Jones' version of finding the location of Göring's treasure is the most logical. Members of the 1269th carefully dug through freshly poured cement, and facing Anderson was an array of art that included *Eve* (Gregor Erhardt, *Belle Allemande*). Anderson had met this beautiful German lady 16 years before at the Louvre. "I was in a daze. I had a momentary flash of skepticism followed quickly by the reality of the situation."[1]

The 1269th reported to Seventh Army Headquarters that they had uncovered the Göring art treasure in Aladdin's Cave, and as a result of this they were placed in charge of guarding the valuables. Anderson protested, and in his zeal said there was even a Cellini bowl in the collection and was asked the question, "What in the hell is Cellini?" Benvenuto Cellini was a sixteenth century goldsmith, sculptor, and painter.

And now the two versions of the stories begin to agree, as Anderson had to take a back seat and the 1269th guarded the treasure. The 40 men of Company A, 2nd Platoon began moving the art from the two large subterranean rooms that were dripping water on to the rich art objects. One crew would haul the objects from the large room and place them in a mine cart. Using a hoist, the cart was pulled to the entrance of the bunker. Here the works of art were offloaded. The smaller silver and *objets d'art* were spread on a tarpaulin on the ground until a large amount was accumulated for the trip to the trucks.

As they were looking at the gold and silver objects on the tarp, Lt. Layton Jones picked up a gold crucifixion of Jesus with Mary and John at the foot of the cross and handed it to his driver, Sgt. Robert L. Thalhofer, with the explanation that he, a Catholic, deserved this as a trophy of war. Thalhofer did not see it that way and declined the offer, as he considered it just plain stealing. Each member of the 2nd Platoon did share in one of the many Reichsmarschall's sterling silver sets. The large hardwood chest engraved with Göring's coat of arms, a bare, muscular arm crooked at the elbow with one finger clutching a ring, contained the complete silver set. Thalhofer selected a single silver pepper shaker.

From the tarp and entrance, the valuables were then carried in a hodge-podge manner up a trail in the forest and loaded into uncovered army trucks. The heavy sculpture was loaded into a wheel barrow with a blanket for padding and transferred to the trucks for the trip to the hotel. It took four days and fifty trips to remove the objects, which were then stored in a requisitioned dry, fireproof hotel at Unterstein once used as a rest center for the Luftwaffe.

Sgt. Thalhofer loaded the trucks and rode the short distance to the hotel. His job was to keep the paintings standing upright and leaning against the sideboards of the truck so they would not flip into each other. On one trip the truck went too fast into a curve and a large painting flipped, ripping a four-inch, three-corner tear in another painting.

During the four days it took to empty the bunker, Layton F. Jones removed a silver-bound copy of *Mein Kampf*. Sergeant Robert Thibodaux removed the baton presented to Göring by Italian Field Marshall Balbo. Thibodaux also walked off with the Göring Wedding Sword, today valued at more than one million dollars. Both items are today in private collections. But the person who collected the incomparable was the commander of the 2nd Platoon, Lieutenant Warren Eckberg, who took a large diamond-encrusted solid-gold medallion hanging from a gold chain, and later he would acquire one of Göring's diamond-studded batons given to him by the Führer.

Members of the Second Platoon of the 1269th Engineer Combat Battalion who helped remove the Göring treasure from a cave near Berchtesgaden (May 1945) were Corporal Van Sellars; PFC Lloyd Mercer; Sergeant Harold Courtney (in charge of recovery of treasure); 1st Lt. Layton F. Jones (discoverer of treasure); Pvt Frank Statile; T5 Oscar C. Allen, Jr.; and PFC Merced Cavazos, Jr.

To house the collection, Capt. Anderson chose the small, modern Bavarian Hotel at Unterstein that had been a rest center for the airmen of the Luftwaffe. The Germans had been removed from the hotel and Company C, 327th Glider Infantry was billeted in the building where the treasures were being stored. The material from the bunker was packed into several rooms.

Major E. U. McRae, Infantry, was assigned the responsibility of safekeeping the Göring treasure. It was difficult, but by May 16th, the major had the soldiers of

A soldier of the 1269th carefully carries a bas relief panel from Aladdin's Cave. The authors believe this is the only photograph of the inside of the underground bunker that contained Göring's vast treasure. *Courtesy National Archives*

Members of the 2nd Platoon, Company A, posing with part of Göring's treasure taken from Aladdin's Cave. In the center, next to the soldier without a shirt, is Lieutenant Layton Jones. The chest held by the shirtless soldier, Harold Courtney, was later turned over to the State of Bavaria with the front broken and some of the valuable stones removed. The painting held by the soldier is Adolf Hitler painted by Karl Rickett, completed in Munich November 12, 1935. *Courtesy of Johnson Reference Books & Militaria.*

The fabulous *objets d'art* of Hermann Göring spread on a tarpaulin at the entrance to Aladdin's Cave. The round baton at the front of the picture was a gift to Reichsmarschall Göring from Italian Field Marshall Italo Balbo. The sword in the case just behind the baton was presented to Göring by General Francisco Franco of Spain. The baton, along with many more of these valuables, was stolen by U.S. soldiers. *Courtesy Ben Curtis Collection*

Captain Harry V. Anderson (right) watches as the Göring art is recovered from Aladdin's Cave. The large painting is Sebastiano Ricco, *Adam and Eve in the Garden of Eden*. *Courtesy National Archives.*

This large oil painting (*Adam and Eve in the Garden of Eden*) is being loaded on a truck. *Courtesy National Archives.*

Lieutenant Kuhn parked beside Göring's train at the Berchtesgaden train station. *Courtesy the Pratt Museum, U.S. Army.*

Some of the Aladdin's Cave treasures are being placed on a truck for transport. Sergeant Harold A. Way (left) and Captain Harry V. Anderson check the load, marking down each item removed from Aladdin's Cave. *Courtesy National Archives.*

C Company moved out. At this time he began to unload the nine freight cars at Unterstein that contained the bulk of Göring's collection. Then he barred the entrances of the doors containing silver and gold items that could easily have been picked up as souvenirs as he reorganized the complete layout of the paintings, furniture, and *objets d'art*.

McRae received orders from Colonel Ned Moore that only people with passes from him and Colonel Harper would be admitted. McRae and his staff spent the rest of the week displaying the booty in the rooms throughout the building. During this time there were parties of sightseers constantly visiting the museum. Guards were kept alerted for souvenir hunters.

On May 14, 1945, Lt. James J. Rorimer and Lt. Calvin Hathaway returned to Berchtesgaden, where they sought out Major Robert S. Smith, head of Military Government (G-5) for the 101st Airborne Division. Rorimer and Hathaway explained to Major Smith General Alexander Patch's concern for the safety of the Göring art collection, and he told them that Captain Harry V. Anderson was hard at work salvaging the collection. Rorimer watched in terror as the untrained soldiers, without any supervision, unloaded the two and a half ton trucks bringing the valuable paintings to the Unterstein Hotel.

The paintings alone filled 40 rooms of the Hotel at Unterstein. Four rooms and a wide corridor door at the end of the ground floor were jammed with

General Maxwell Taylor, General Omar Bradley, and Colonel Harper view Göring's private train in the Berchtesgaden railroad yards. *Courtesy the Pratt Museum, U.S. Army.*

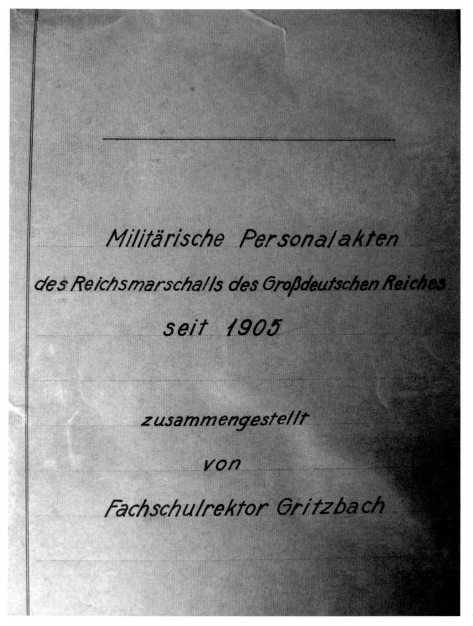

Militärische Personalakten

des Reichsmarschalls des Großdeutschen Reiches

seit 1905

zusammengestellt

von

Fachschulrektor Gritzbach

Documents taken from the Göring train by T-Force. The cover reads "Military Personal Documents of the Reichsmarschall of the Greater German Reich – since 1905, arranged by school administrator Gritzbach." *Courtesy U.S. Army Military History Institute.*

Major McRae's soldiers of the 101st unpack these valuables from the train's baggage cars. These two Madonnas came from South Germany. The crowned Madonna and child on the right, a fifteenth century piece, stands on a half moon. The statue on the left carried by the soldiers is from the sixteenth century. In the back of the train are stacked paintings awaiting removal. (Courtesy National Archives)

sculpture. Three rooms were crammed with barrels, boxes, and trunks full of porcelain*. Still another room was piled high with tapestries. In another room there were 70 cases of books consisting of 11,000 books and pamphlets. Two rooms, numbered five and eight, were referred to as the gold rooms and were padlocked, as they contained many small silver and gold items, including several ceremonial swords that had been presented to Göring. A small chapel on the premise was overflowing with Italian Renaissance furniture. The condition of the art objects was excellent, except that many items from Göring's collection contained scratches and some bullet holes. Göring's collection of art work, the crème de la crème, consisted of approximately 1,000 paintings, 80 pieces of sculpture, 60 tapestries, and 2,600 gold, silver, and gem encrusted *objets d'art*.

Rorimer began an inspection of the art objects, but almost immediately received word that General Maxwell Taylor wanted him to come to his headquarters with Major Smith for a discussion of the Göring art. Rorimer welcomed the chance, and told the General about the lack of security and hodge-podge handling of the art. Taylor immediately assigned some troops for security duties and delegated Captain Anderson full time to supervising and assembling the Göring art collection. The General told Rorimer that he wanted the Monuments, Fine Art and Archival section to take the Göring collection from his area of responsibility as soon as possible. He also made arrangements for the arrest of Hofer and his wife, Bertha, so they could be under observation and work with the collection. Bertha was to administer first aid, but not repaint or restore missing parts to the canvases that had been damaged. Mr. and Mrs. Hofer and their daughter

Here is a view of part of Göring's collection. The figurines, candelabras, and goblets are made of gold-plated silver. In the foreground is the sword presented to Göring by General Franco that had been moved from the tarp in a previous photo to the Unterstein Hotel. The sword, turned over to the U.S. Army in 1952, is missing. *Courtesy National Archives.*

* Porcelain, commonly referred to as china by most English speaking people, is universally admired and highly collectable. The reference is because porcelain was first made by the Chinese.

Some of the treasures stored in Gold Room number five. The sword in the center foreground is the gold sword presented to Göring by Italian Dictator Benito Mussolini. Note the silver Luftwaffe Pokal (Göring's?) beside the sword. *Courtesy National Archives.*

Lieutenant Gordon Rohrbacher of St. Paul, Minnesota, along with some of the valuables in the Gold Room, is examining the sword presented to Göring by Benito Mussolini. *Courtesy of Johnson Reference Books & Militaria.*

One of the 40 rooms stuffed with sculpture. The white figure on the left is Luca Della Robbia's *Mary Magdalena and the Urn*. In the center are *Madonna* and *Angel of Renunciation*. *Courtesy National Archives.*

Priceless Oriental carpets looted from occupied Europe were taken from Aladdin's Cave. An American sentry is shown standing guard over a portion of the art treasures set aside by Göring for the gallery he planned to build at Carinhall. *Courtesy National Archives.*

Sergeant R. N. Snook of Elmyra, Arkansas, examines an alabaster hunting horn embossed in silver. He is surrounded by pieces of silver of great antique value. *Courtesy National Archives.*

Walter Andres Hofer holds one of the many priceless oils acquired by Göring. In the center is Cranach's *Rest on the Flight into Egypt*, which Hofer is discussing with Major E.U. McRae of Valdosta, Georgia. McRae was the initial custodian for the Göring treasure. *Courtesy National Archives.*

Colonel Harper and General Taylor examine books and documents in the underground store rooms near Hitler's Berghof in Obersalzberg. *Courtesy the Pratt Museum, U.S. Army.*

Göring's priceless art collection was one of the top attractions, along with the homes once occupied by high ranking officials of the Nazi party at Obersalzberg. The Mercedes parked in front of the museum had been filched by General Alexander Patch, Commander of the Seventh Army. This visit gave credence to the made-up story that Patch had taken Göring's baton from the exhibit. The sign advertising the art collection is today in the collection of noted Texas collector Mike Morris. *Courtesy National Archives.*

Bertha Hofer makes restorations on Velazques' *Infanta Margareta* while in Berchtesgaden under house arrest. The painting was seized from the Rothschild collection in Paris. Beneath the table, left, is Rembrandt's *Young Boy with a Hat. Courtesy National Archives.*

moved into the Hotel at Unterstein to take up the work of arranging the art and repairing it.

Later that same day, May 15th, Rorimer, Hathaway and Hofer spent several hours looking through the cars of Göring's three trains, now in different locations. Göring's ten-car personal train contained huge bedrooms with dressing rooms and giant double beds, dining rooms, military offices, and even a recreation car. There were drawers of medals set with rubies, emeralds, and diamonds. One of the ten cars had been filled with champagne, scotch, and other fine liquors. Everything was strewn about with papers everywhere, even thrown out of the windows. The trains had been thoroughly looted a week earlier, with the French

Army Intelligence arriving first and removing the more valuable documents. Rorimer had soldiers from the 101st guard the trains as Lieutenant Hathaway and four soldiers searched the trains looking for documents that pertained to Göring's art collection. It took two days to gather the following papers:

> Art Exchange with Eugenio Ventura (Italy); correspondence with Walter Andreas Hofer; correspondence with Werner Peiner and Gisela Limberger; financial records, bank receipts, personal calendar, gifts received (1936-1944), jewelry collections, notes on purchases, paintings, and inventory from Veldenstein; papers, Chronological (1940-1944); papers, numerically sequenced (nos. 1-3605); and receipts for art objects (July 1940-October 1944)

These documents were placed in a steel filing cabinet equipped with a lock and placed in the custody of Captain Anderson. A week later Rorimer and Hathaway went to analyze the documents, but were refused permission to review them. After considerable quibbling the documents were turned over to Rorimer of the Monuments, Fine Art and Archival Section. Meanwhile, Capt. Harry V. Anderson had searched through the cabinet of material and removed Göring's 50th birthday list and Dr. Eduard Plietzach's letter of June 7, 1942, describing valuable art that was available on the Dutch art market. These documents are today in the possession of Mike Morris (The documents taken from the train by Rorimer are today in the National Archives and available online at footnote. com.)

During Rorimer's activity with the train, T-Force also removed thousands of documents from the train that included two large, Russian, loose-leaf atlases; also a secret photo album of the German Fifth Luftwaffe during its operations in Norway, an autographed pamphlet by Sven Tunberg, a catalogue of old paintings in connection with Göring's art treasures, and four folders of names and addresses concerning SS leaders. Overall 11,000 books were removed from the train. Thousands of these maps, books, and photo albums are today in the Library of Congress. Four framed photographs are today in the Library of Congress: the mother of Göring, his wife, his first wife Carin, and a silver and gold-coated frame embedded with lapis lazuli with the photo of his wife and child.

Göring's World War I records and many of the letters from Göring's first wife, Carin, were removed and are today archived in the U.S. Army Military History Institute, Carlisle, Pennsylvania. In one of the documents a bit of humor regarding the ridiculousness of the early Nazi Party beginnings is revealed. Carin writes her Swedish mother that Hitler has written a book, *Four and a Half Years; Battles Against Lies, Cowardice, and Stupidity,* and expected the sales to yield millions, thus rescuing the Görings from their poverty. Carin assumed that Hitler was obligated to Hermann, who had sacrificed himself completely for the betterment of the Nazi party. Before the press release, the title of the book was changed to *Mein Kampf* (My Struggle) by Max Amann, the multimillionaire German publisher. While searching through this and other material on the Göring train, Intelligence Officer George Allen reported, "He found enough drugs in the bedroom of the train to kill about 30 men."[2]

Also taken from the train was an extensive personal collection of photographs of Hermann Göring, as he had given instructions for his office staff to collect and organize a series of albums of all available photographs of him. His staff assembled photographs submitted by the news agencies, informal snapshots of family outings and hunting parties, and close-ups of conversational interludes. They then selected the significant ones, event by event, covering the years 1933-1942. The photo album ended here, with several volumes missing. One album contains an amazing collection formed by Göring as an aviator in the First World War, showing Göring and his associates in the minutest detail. A set of pictures of Göring's country castle in Neuhaus is also among the many German documentary series. The photo albums attest to little that has not been written by biographers concerning Göring. But what we already know is reinforced by this intimate record of the meetings he attended, the accolades accorded him on his birthday, the sport cars he tried out, the vacations he enjoyed, and the men and women who surrounded him. In all, there are an estimated 18,500 photographs in 47 albums. Most of these albums are today in the Library of Congress.

Major E.U. McRae had assumed responsibility for the Hermann Göring treasure, and on Saturday, May 19th, he ordered that the gold and silver be moved from various rooms in the hotel to the three rooms in the main hall downstairs, and he fixed the doors so they could be locked. At the same time Hofer, his wife, and their small daughter moved into the hotel to take up the work of arranging the art and making minor repairs. McRae reported that the next day, Sunday, Major White [sic Smith] and Captain Anderson brought 18 correspondents out, and they interviewed Mr. Hofer and took a number of pictures. During the day, someone cut about a three inch square out of one of the paintings. Due to the great number of visitors (about 500), it was impossible to determine who did it. McRae requested that they discontinue giving passes to large parties.

That Sunday Judy Barden, Correspondent for the *New York Sun*, was one of the visitors, and reported she was escorted by Major Robert S. Smith, Captain Harry V. Anderson, and Lieutenant James J. Rorimer, curator of the medieval art department of the Metropolitan Museum of Art. Of most interest, she writes, "On leaving the building, I took a quick look through the Nazi Air Marshal's heavy book, and among various visitors who signed their names were Charles and Ann Lindbergh on July 28, 1937, and the Duke and Duchess of Windsor on October 19, 1937. Hitler had the whole first page to himself. When Major Smith saw what Wallis, Duchess of Windsor, had written, he remarked with a wicked twinkle in his eye, 'That Baltimore gal really went to town, didn't she.'" *What makes this interesting – this signature book was taken by General Maxwell Taylor as a souvenir.*

Lieutenant James J. Rorimer was busy elsewhere. Therefore, on May 21st (Whit Monday), the date supplied by Calvin Hathaway, Captain Harry Anderson and Thomas C. Howe, MFA&A Officer, went to Fischhorn Castle and presented papers to Emmy Göring identifying themselves as Fine Art Officers. The MFA&A officers took some of Emmy's seven nest-egg items: (4) four small Angel Musicians paintings, by Hans Memling; (5) Vermeer/Van Meegeren *Christ with the Woman Taken in Adultery*; (6) Roger van der Weyden, *Madonna with Child*; and the (7) Renders' Memling, *Madonna with Child*. Göring had taken the Renders painting from Carinhall in a red velvet-lined box that served as its frame, and had given it to Emmy Göring, who had placed the painting with her personal belongings. She had taken it to Mauterndorf Castle, where Göring removed it from the velvet-lined box. Emmy then took the "unframed" painting, along with eight other paintings, with her to Fischhorn Castle. Mrs. Göring denied any knowledge of the Vermeer/van Meegeren, but finally Christa Gormanns brought the painting from its hiding place wrapped around a stove pipe. She said "Guard this carefully, it is of great value." Mrs. Göring wept bitterly as the paintings were removed. Captain Anderson made out a receipt for the paintings and, according to a Memorandum of Conversation, Captain Anderson did not list the paintings by artist "because he didn't know one painter from the other."[4] Two of the four small Angels disappeared on the day and were never recovered.

The night of May 21st, after McRae had left the museum for the day, Captain Anderson removed four small paintings. The next morning two of the pictures were missing. McRae investigated and made out a report of the missing paintings. The final paragraph of McRae's May 27, 1945, report concluded, "I do not believe that, with the exception of the malicious damage to one picture and disappearance of two small pictures, there have been any serious damage

Tec/4 Richard S. Peck, a college art teacher at Ohio State before the war, acted as guide for the collection and compiled an inventory. *Courtesy Pratt Museum, U.S. Army.*

Miss Patricia Lochridge, the attractive 29-year-old reporter for CBS Radio, and Captain Harry Anderson pose with a controversial paintings acquired by Hermann Göring, Vermeer's *Christ with the Woman Taken in Adultery*. This painting, along with seven more, were taken from Emmy Göring on May 21st while she was staying at Fischhorn Castle. This painting was removed from its hiding place wrapped around a stove pipe. Later the above painting was proven to be a fake painted by Hans van Meegeren, who collected three million dollars for the fake painting in 1942 dollars. Three of the Hans Memling paintings taken that day by Anderson disappeared immediately. Still missing today, these paintings would fetch millions. *Courtesy National Archives.*

to pictures nor have there been any of the treasures lost." During this week of May 20th to May 27th, McRea's team completed unloading the freight cars, distributed fire extinguishers throughout the building, procured a fire detachment, made a better arrangement of Göring's personal articles, and conducted numerous tours for distinguished guests. They also began the installation of chains across all doors to better protect the paintings from damage. Up to this present time no inventory or cataloging had been accomplished because of the numerous interruptions by people requesting Hofer for a guide.

Anderson was involved in day-to-day activities, for on the night of May 22nd, Lieutenant William S. Scheuer, Interrogation Center, Seventh Army requested a Military Government representative of the 101st Airborne meet him in St. Johann, Austria, as that village was in their occupation zone. The following morning Captain Harry V. Anderson met Scheuer, who had in his custody General Gottlieb Berger, who had been in charge of Germany's Prisoner of War Administration and was earlier captured by the 101st. During a routine interrogation, Berger stated that he had worked directly under Heinrich Himmler, who had given him money to hide. Berger said the money was the property of the Reichsbank, not his nor Himmler's, and offered to show the Americans where he buried it. That morning General Berger led Anderson and Scheuer to the chief forester's home, which was connected to a barn. They removed some floorboards in the barn, dug down four feet, and removed eight large cloth sacks and one large metal box. The sacks and box contained a million dollars' worth of currency from 25 different countries. There was no U.S. currency in this cache. The currency was turned over to the 101st Division Finance Officer and later sent to the U.S. Foreign Exchange Depository as shipment number 27D.

Beginning about June 4th, Captain Anderson took official command of safeguarding the Göring treasure and appointed Tec/4 Edward S. Peck to act as a guide and curator for the valuables stored in the Hotel at Unterstein. The 37-year-old Peck was well qualified, as he had been a professor of fine arts in Oberlin College prior to joining the Army in 1942. He had been with the 101st Airborne since its inception and had been awarded a Purple Heart for wounds sustained in Holland. On July 9th, under orders from Anderson, Peck, PFC Lawrence Olin, and Hofer and his wife, Bertha, compiled a descriptive inventory of the collection. The inventory was typed by PFC Robert B. Herriot.

On July 21, 1945, the MFA&A team of Thomas Howe, Lamont Moore, and Steve Kovalyak arrived at Unterstein and contacted Captain Harry Anderson. They were here to remove Göring's treasure as requested by General Maxwell Taylor on May 15th. They then sat down and discussed moving the objects with Captain Anderson and Tech 4 Richard S. Peck, who had compiled a 72-page inventory of the complete collection that would be sent to the Munich Central Collection Center.

Howe requested a work party of U.S. soldiers to help pack the Göring treasure and suggested they ask for volunteers who had an interest in art objects. Eight soldiers from Battery D, 468th AAA volunteered. They were Tec/5 Vitello, Tec/5 Wilson M. Halena, PFC Les H. Hoffman, PFC Wilford Starrett, PFC Raymond Snyder, PFC Wallace G. Bert, Pvt. Dean Ponak, and Pvt. Leo McKinley.

The following day, the team had their first four trucks loaded for the 90-mile trip to the Munich Central Collection Point. One of the last objects packed was the *Belle Allemande*, the work of art that had been owned by the Louvre. Howe and Moore admired the statue of the beautiful nude German and fancied that Göring detected a resemblance between the statue and his wife Emmy.

On July 29th – a Sunday afternoon – the MFA&A team turned their attention to the gold room on the ground floor. There were gold chalices studded with precious stones, silver tankards, reliquaries of gold and enamel work, boxes of Jade and malachite, candelabras, clocks and lamps of marble and gold, precious plaques of carved ivory, and sets of table ornaments. A few of the items were equipped with leather cases. There was also a gold baton with precious stones, a present from the Luftwaffe. Howe wrote:

> Towards the end of the afternoon [Sunday, July 29th] we were waited on by a delegation of three officers from the 101st Airborne Division. They had come to inquire if we would consider turning over to them the gold sword that Mussolini had given to Göring. They wanted it as a trophy for a club of the 101st Airborne officers that they were going to organize. They planed to set up a club room when they got home and have annual reunions. The swords they said would be an appropriate souvenir. I told them that I had been directed to ship everything to Munich and did not have authority to make other dispositions of objects in the collection. But since the sword could not be regarded as a cultural object – a fact which I called to their attention – I suggested they take the matter up with Third Army Headquarters in Munich. I refrained from informing them that, for all of me, they could have their pick of modern objects in the gold room.

Howe (the Monuments, Fine Art and Archival Officer) and his staff stuffed 1,950 *objets d'art* items into 22 cabinets and sent these valuables to the Munich Central Collection Center. On August 4, 1945 – after 13 days – the Göring Collection, including 1,012 paintings, 263 sculptures, 81 tapestries, and 166 cases that included 41 large crates of books, had been moved in 32 truckloads from the three-story hotel at Unterstein to the Munich Central Collection Point.

John Walker, Chief Curator National Gallery Art, Washington, DC, and Major Bancel La Farge, Chief MFA&A behind the Unterstein Hotel. Note the wooden packing crates that would be used in packing the Göring treasure. *Courtesy National Archives.*

On Walker's and La Farge's visit to Berchtesgaden, Anderson, right, suggested they visit the Eagle's Nest. The officer in the Naval uniform is Thomas Carr Howe, who was in charge of moving the Göring treasure to Munich. *Courtesy National Archives.*

The U.S. Army appropriated the elegant Nazi buildings in the Berchtesgaden area. While assigned to Berchtesgaden, Thomas Carr Howe stayed at the Berchtesgadener Hof, the official residence for U.S. officers. Howe took this business card as a souvenir. Major Richard "Dick" D. Winters of *Band of Brothers* fame took a four-foot long velvet case of silverware from this elegant hotel. *Courtesy National Archives.*

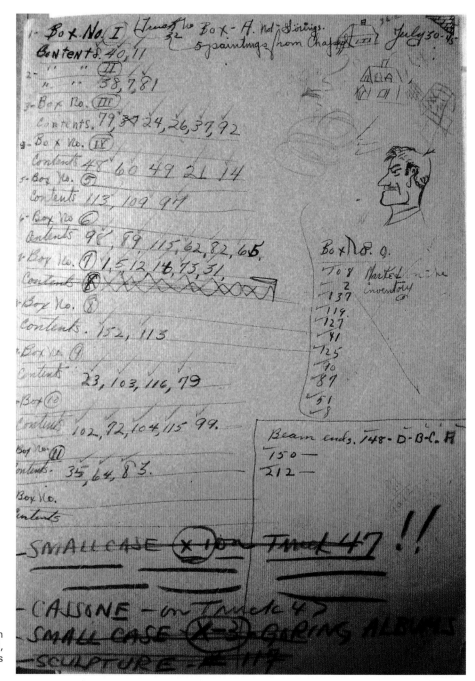

A summary of the last shipment of inventory from the Göring Collection. The top is dated "July 30, 45," and this artwork is most likely from Thomas Carr Howe. *Courtesy National Archives.*

568-43

Berchtesgaden

DATE	NAME	ADDRESS
2, May 45	Wade H. Haislip	Lt. General Hq XV Corps
	Burton K. Wheeler	U S Senator Montana
	Homer Capehart	U. S. Senator Indiana
	Paul A. Porter	Federal Communications Commission
	Joseph R. Redman	Rear Admiral U S Navy.
	Carroll O. Bickelhaupt	Brig. Gen. U.S. Army
	Frank E Stoner	Maj. Gen., U. S Army.
5/26/45	A. W. Hawkes	US Sen. New Jersey U.S.A.
	Ernest W. McFarland	US Sen Arizona U. S. A
	Guy Gatch	
	Bemow Mattern	Lt. Col. PRD, SHAEF
	Burnet R. Maybank	U.S.S. South Carolina

The guest book of the 101st is replete with important dignitaries visiting Berchtesgaden, as noted by the Generals' and Senators' signatures at the top. The bottom image is page one of this guest book and contains the signatures of Winston Churchill, Dwight Eisenhower, and Omar Bradley. *Courtesy Pratt Museum, U.S. Army.*

DATE	NAME	ADDRESS
	Winston S. Churchill	10 Downing Street, London
	Dwight D Eisenhower	Abilene. Kansas.
	Omar Bradley,	Moberly Mo.
	Lewis H Brereton	Annapolis Md
	Ralph Royce	Hancock Michigan
	Paul L. Williams	Los Angeles, Calif
	Sarah J. Riner.	London.
	M. B. Ridgway	Washington D C Maj. Gen
	Chet Holifield	19th District of California

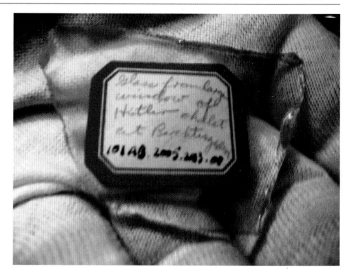

Sightseers looking from what was the large glass window at Hitler's Berchtesgaden home. The window could be lowered to allow the pure alpine air to circulate throughout the entire chalet. *Courtesy Pratt Museum, U.S. Army.* Unbelievably (right), a soldier brought a piece of this broken glass home as a souvenir. *Courtesy Pratt Museum, U.S. Army.*

Time off for these soldiers of the 101st as they enjoy Berchtesgaden and nearby Koenig's Lake. Guard duty of the electric boats was a desired assignment (left). Unfortunately a policy of no fraternization was enforced, and these men of the 101st can only observe this shapely Fraulein swing her way up the walkway to their rest center. *Courtesy Pratt Museum, U.S. Army.*

The soldiers of the 101st Airborne spent three of the best months of their lives in Berchtesgaden, living in the scrumptious homes of the big wigs of the Third Reich, and then realism set in when the unit was shipped back to France in September 1945. They arrived in Auxerre in these French boxcars marked on the side "40 Hommes 8 Chevaux" (40 Men or 8 Horses), with straw as bedding. The old French army barracks where the men were quartered were naturally in bad shape from the hard usage of the war years and quite a contrast from the recent tourist hotels, inns, and homes of Germany and Austria. The 101st was deactivated in France, and the men returned to the United States by year's end. *Courtesy of Pratt Museum, United States Army.*

11
Looting the Reichsmarschall Booty

Rules of Land Warfare
War Department, Washington DC,
Field Manual 27-10

326. Confiscation. – Private property cannot be confiscated.

327. Booty. – All captures and booty belong, according to modern law of war, primarily to the government of the captor.

328. Private gains by officers or soldiers prohibited. Neither officers nor soldiers are allowed to make use of their position of power in the hostile country for private gains, not even for commercial transactions otherwise legitimate.

As far as booty is concerned regarding item 327 above, the U.S. War Department declared on August 31, 1944, that captured equipment may be retained as war trophies. This declaration, known as Circular 6, stipulated the individual's trophy value should exceed the salvage value, and the trophy's owner had a certificate signed by his superior officer that he was officially authorized to retain the award. Then, in the closing days of World War II, the European Theater of Command's Military Government Law declared the Nazi Party illegal and its property subject to seizure, and to be taken into possession of the Military Government. In some convoluted way this Nazi Party property generally came to be considered in the same status as captured enemy military equipment. This conclusion was widespread among the high-ranking officers of the European Command, as it gave then "legal" status to reach into a large pool of booty trophies.

Between May 22nd and prior to the arrival of the MFA&A officers on July 21, 1945, many of the items stored in the Unterstein Hotel were filched. The exact sequence of events regarding the looting of the valuables in the Unterstein Hotel is unknown, but the following has been reconstructed from various sources, including the *Daily Diary* entry from June 2, 1945:

> Col Wilson, 106 Cav Gp, arrived at the Division Command Post with Queen of Belgium. Col Moore entertained her at tea after which she was shown the Göring collection. She did not remove anything from the collection.

This is an amazing statement, for on June 2nd, nine U.S. Senators, including Harry Byrd from Virginia and several ranking generals, including Brigadier General Kenneth Royall, were met at Salzburg and toured Berchtesgaden. Was it permissible for them to select souvenirs from the Göring trove?

On this day apparently, Princess Lilian of Belgium did not take advantage of the situation, but she disapproved of Hofer and his wife's activities and reported they were doing more harm than good, and should not be allowed to touch the collection. The *Daily Diary* during this time is replete with more important visitors.

Texas-born war correspondent Miss Patricia Lochridge arrived in all this excitement. The attractive 29-year-old was a reporter for CBS Radio, and she left the Unterstein Hotel with a large, valuable Lucas Cranach painting from the Göring collection. Her son said she had been told [by Major Robert S. Smith] she could help herself from a warehouse [Unterstein Hotel] full of art. Miss Lochridge also took one of Göring's sashes and turned it into a hat and handbag.

While not in the spirit of Circular 6, General Maxwell Taylor made the command decision to classify Göring's treasure as "war trophies." A large number of Göring's valuables were then taken as trophies. Among these souvenirs were twelve large silver goblets taken from the collection. These cups contained a design of both Hermann Göring's and his wife's coat of arms. The cups were taken to a German jeweler to be inscribed with the names of higher ranking soldiers of the 101st Airborne Division. Thirty-six smaller, silver cups were also taken from the Göring collection and presented to all primary staff officers, regimental commanders, and separate battalion commanders. They were presented as courtesy of Hermann Göring and Major General Taylor. These 36 cups were entrusted to a sergeant to be taken to the German jeweler for engraving, but the sergeant only had 35 engraved, keeping one for himself. In later years he sold this engraved cup to Ben Curtis.

In Berchtesgaden, the higher ranking officers of the 101st were:

> General Maxwell Taylor, Division Commander – later he was appointed Ambassador to Vietnam, and in that capacity was given "command decisions" of U.S. Forces. After a stormy one year tenure he was relieved of that position.
> General Gerald Higgins, Assistant Division Commander
> Lieutenant Colonel Ned Moore, G-1 – Personnel, - remained in the army and retired as a Major General.
> Lieutenant Colonel Paul A. Danahy, G-2 – Intelligence
> Lieutenant Colonel H.W.O. Kinnard, G-3 – Operation, retired September 1, 1969, as Commanding General of Fort Belvior, Virginia
> Lieutenant Colonel Carl W. Kohls, G-4 – Supply
> Major Robert S. Smith, G-5 – Military Government, returned to practice law in Indianapolis.
> Lieutenant Colonel David Gold, Surgeon
> Lieutenant Colonel Julian J. Ewell, Commander 501st Airborne Infantry Regiment

Lieutenant Colonel Steve Chappuis, Commander 502nd Airborne
    Infantry Regiment – retired from the army in 1962 as a
    Brigadier General
Lieutenant Colonel Robert F. Sink, Commander 506th Airborne
    Infantry Regiment, popularized in the *Band of Brothers* series.
Colonel Joseph H. Harper, Commander 327th Glider Infantry
    Regiment, retired from the army as a Major General in 1959.
    Born in 1901, he died August 8, 1990.

Among the vast array of items taken was the Göring guest book. It was "awarded' to General Taylor. Lieutenant Warren Eckberg walked off with the aforementioned diamond encrusted baton. Hundreds of expensive Sèvres porcelain china pieces were taken, including a large serving dish that is today in the estate of General Maxwell Taylor.

Regarding this booty collection, Texan collector Ben Curtis recalls that General Ned Moore told him the following:

> Maxwell Taylor had control of the contents, and on his staff was a Colonel that was the chemical warfare expert. Since there was no chemical warfare going on he was not very busy, so at the end of the conflict, Taylor had this Colonel load up a large amount of plundered items from the Cave [Hotel at Unterstein] and other places onto a plane and take it to his home in Bryn Mawr, Pennsylvania. After the war, Taylor and some of his staff met at this Colonel's home and spit up the loot. Taylor took most of the good stuff, and it is this family [Taylor] I was telling you about that still had a lot of the items. This was told to me by Gen. Ned Moore, who was on the staff and was one of the Colonels that met at the home. He even called Taylor's son for me to see if he would sell, and the son said "not at this time." Moore said he had eaten off of Hitler's or Göring's China at Taylor's home.

Purchased by Ben Curtis and his partner Texan, Ben Swearingen, were a silver chest and a gold coated swastika eagle decorated with army life scenes purchased from General Ned Moore. A silver cigar box was purchased from Captain Harry V. Anderson. Swearingen also purchased the most prized possession of his career, Göring's ceremonial hunting knife. It was purchased from Lula White, the widow of the aforementioned Lieutenant Colonel Willard White, as he had divorced Josefa Johnson in 1950. In the late 1970s, Swearingen paid the widow, now living in Arizona, more than $40,000 for the knife. He also bought a 32-piece set of Sèvres porcelain with Göring's coat of arms and 25 pieces of silverware with Hitler's crest.

When Colonel Joseph H. Harper died, two men representing the 101st Don F. Pratt Museum went to Harper's home and told his widow that it had been Harper's intention to present his trophies to that museum. They were driving a U-Haul truck, which they filled with the valuables and then disappeared. It has been reported that one of the men was from Michigan and went by the name Langtree, and the other was the former secretary of the 101st Airborne Division Association. After a lengthy legal battle that no one will discuss, some of Harper's items were sent to the Pratt Museum, including several chairs removed from Hitler's Berghof.

The large silver baton studded with intertwining rows of turquoise with a tear shaped piece of carved ivory at one end is today owned by famed German militaria collector Ben Curtis. *Courtesy Kenneth D. Alford.*

The baton in the hands of Sgt. Robert Thibodaux, 1269th Combat Engineers, was presented to Göring by Italian Air Marshall Italo Balbo. Thibodaux was posing at the entrance of Aladdin's Cave. A few days later Col. Willard White would possess the baton. *Courtesy Ben Curtis Collection.*

Lt. Warren H. Eckberg was awarded Hermann Göring's treasured baton, above, that was inscribed: "[From] the Führer to the First Fieldmarschall of the Air Force." The top of the baton, above left, contains a wreath and German Eagle made from 20 diamonds. The base is silver with black enamel bearing the Iron Cross. *Courtesy of Kenneth D. Alford.*

Another valuable item granted to Eckberg (right) had been presented to Hermann Göring by the Carol-Wilhelminia Institute. It was a solid gold medallion hanging from a gold chain a ½ inch wide. The face of the oval medallion contained a crystal enameled coat of arms rimmed with 60 small diamonds. *Courtesy of Kenneth D. Alford.*

Lt. Eckberg mailed these items home to his mother in Chicago while he remained in Europe. He requested that she hold the valuables, but she ran this classified ad in a Chicago newspaper for the sale of the medallion. A jeweler contacted Eckberg's mother and she presented him with the medallion. The jeweler contacted U.S. Customs, who took them into custody because Eckberg had failed to comply with customs regulations and could not prove lawful possession. These items are on display at the National Infantry Museum, Fort Benning, Georgia. *Courtesy of Kenneth D. Alford.*

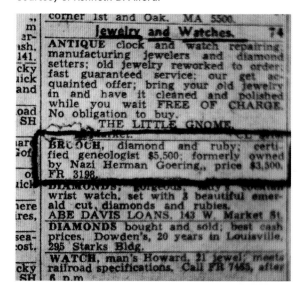

The most informed collectors and soldiers involved with the Göring treasure believe this baton was taken from Aladdin's Cave. It has taken on a life of its own and is just not true. Göring is carrying this Luftwaffe baton in a green felt cloth in his left hand as he surrenders at the Seventh Army Interrogation Center in Augsburg, Germany. The baton was taken by General Arthur White from Göring and presented to General Alexander Patch, the Commander of the Seventh Army. On March 23, 1946, his widow presented the baton to the West Point Military Museum. In preservation instinct, Captain Harry Anderson wrote, "General Patch stole the Göring baton from the collection and gave it to Harry Truman, momentarily jeopardizing my career. My creditability was restored as soon as General Patch was disclosed as the culprit." *Courtesy National Archives.*

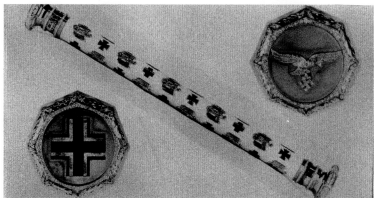

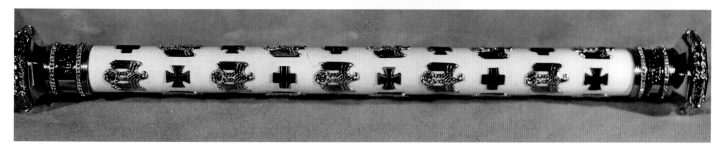

The first item on evaluation inventory was this guest book presented to Hermann and Emmy Göring as a wedding present on April 10, 1935, by the Prussian Council of State. The first page contains this note, dated Berlin, 10 April 1935, "With the most cordial wishes for happiness and bliss," and is signed by Adolf Hitler. The guest book, bound in silver, was kept in Carinhall and contained the signatures of many distinguished guests. The book was taken by the Commanding General of the 101st Airborne Division, General Maxwell Taylor. He erroneously reported the book was taken from the Luftwaffe Headquarters in Berchtesgaden and presented to him. Following World War II, General Taylor was appointed as Superintendent of the U.S. Military Academy at West Point. After considerable investigation by the U.S. Military Academy Museum the guest book was donated by General Taylor to that museum in May 1948. *Courtesy Kenneth D. Alford*

Göring's eleven pound silver presentation platter has 96 star rubies around the outer edge. The center has the Luftwaffe Eagle with sun rays and a Ju88 and Me109 soaring from the center. Collector Mike Morris purchased this platter from a Los Angeles trade fair in 1992. *Courtesy Mike Morris*

This silver cup and platter were taken by General Maxwell Taylor from Berchtesgaden as a souvenir. *Courtesy of Johnson Reference Books & Militaria.*

This Sèvres porcelain serving platter is today in the collection of General Maxwell Taylor' estate. It is one of many taken by the officers of the 101st Airborne. The back (right photo) of all the Sèvres porcelain taken at Berchtesgaden was engraved "The Reichsmarschall of the Greater German Reiches, Hermann Göring on his 50th Birthday, 12 January 1943." *Courtesy of Johnson Reference Books & Militaria.*

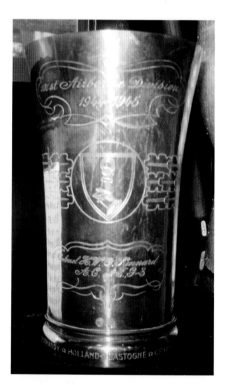

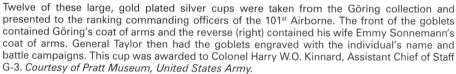

Twelve of these large, gold plated silver cups were taken from the Göring collection and presented to the ranking commanding officers of the 101st Airborne. The front of the goblets contained Göring's coat of arms and the reverse (right) contained his wife Emmy Sonnemann's coat of arms. General Taylor then had the goblets engraved with the individual's name and battle campaigns. This cup was awarded to Colonel Harry W.O. Kinnard, Assistant Chief of Staff G-3. *Courtesy of Pratt Museum, United States Army.*

Thirty-six of these large engraved silver cups with Göring's coat of arms were presented to the primary staff officers, regimental commanders, and battalion commanders of the 101st Airborne Division. Three of these cups are today in the Don F. Pratt Museum in Fort Campbell, Kentucky, home of the 101st Airborne Division. The above was donated to the museum by the widow of Lt. Col. William Steward. *Courtesy of Pratt Museum, United States Army.*

This gold plated silver cup commissioned by Göring as Master of the Greater German Reich Forests was taken by Lieutenant Colonel Stewart and donated to the Pratt Museum. *Courtesy of Pratt Museum, United States Army.*

This Order of the Crown of Italy, with the complimentary wearing medal, missing the ribbon, was presented to the 101st Pratt Museum by the widow of William R. Stewart. It was wrongly classified as the Star of Italy. The presentation of this medal was reportedly made to Göring on May 23, 1939, at the signing of the Pact of Steel by Italian Foreign Minister Ciano. *Courtesy Pratt Museum, U.S. Army.*

Constanzo Ciano does not mention this award in his diary, but writes that German Minister Joachim von Ribbentrop was awarded the Supreme Order of the Most Holy Annunciation, the pinnacle of the honors system in the Kingdom of Italy. He then scornfully writes: "Göring had tears in his eyes when he saw the collar of the Annunziata around the neck of Ribbentrop." Concerning Göring's 50th birthday, Ciano entry in his diary, "Göring, to whom Martin Franklin [Italian Ambassador] today handed the first Gold Star of the Roman Eagle, expressed his thanks so vociferously that his childish joy was obvious."

Patricia Lochridge took one of Göring's Cranach paintings, similar to this masterpiece of Cupid complaining to Venus about being stung by bees when stealing a honeycomb. This is to be taken as a moral commentary, as the inscription observes, "life's pleasure is mixed with pain." The painting was purchased from a New York art dealer by the National Gallery, London, in 1963 for 34,000 British Pounds, then a whopping $120,000. *Courtesy National Archives.*

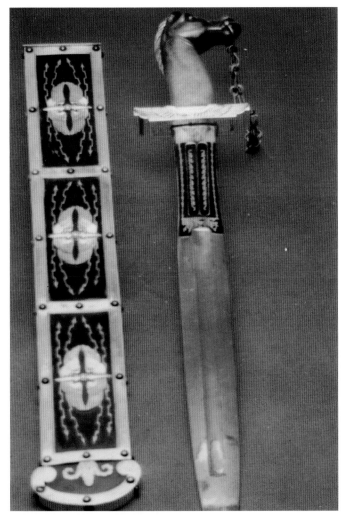

This French deluxe ceremonial Roman Gladius style sword was crafted by Napoleon's personal armoire. John C. Porter retrieved this valuable blade from Göring's Obersalzberg reflective pool, apparently blown there by the bombing of his chalet. William C. Blynn purchased this most unique sword in 1978 for an undisclosed amount. Most unfortunately the blade has since been ruined by moisture while it remained in the scabbard. *Courtesy of Johnson Reference Books & Militaria.*

This incredible hunting dagger was purchased from Lieutenant Colonel Willard White's widow in 1976 by Ben Swearingen and his partner Ben Curtis for $40,000. It was sold to deceased collector Roger Steel. It is today in a private collection. *Courtesy of Johnson Reference Books & Militaria.*

This candid photo taken at Carinhall depicts Göring wearing this incredible hunting dagger. *Courtesy of Johnson Reference Books & Militaria.*

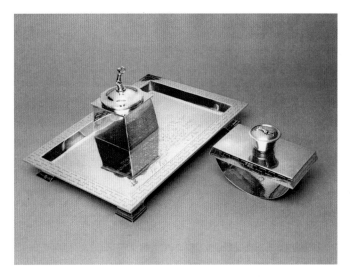

Göring's outstanding desk set and blotter is today owned by Mike and Mark Chenault. The silver blotter was made by Berlin Silversmith H.J. Wilms. *Courtesy Mike and Mark Chenault.*

12
The Munich Central Collection Point

Immediately following hostilities, the U.S. Army established four Collection Points for art objects and other cultural material that had been discovered in the U.S. Zone of Occupation. They were located in Munich, Marburg, Wiesbaden, and Offenbach. The Collection Points housed cultural material requiring evacuation because of inadequate storage conditions or insufficient security, and most importantly cultural material suspected of having been looted by the Germans from occupied countries.

Of these four Collection Points, the one in Munich was the largest and its operation was the most complex. By reason of the vast amount of looted art objects in Bavaria and Austria, the urgent need for a large central collection center was felt early in the occupation of Germany. A preliminary survey revealed that two enormous, three-story Nazi Party buildings (the *Verwaltungsbau* and the *Führerbau* in Munich) were admirably suited for this purpose. These two adjoining landmark buildings, renamed Galley I and Galley II, were requisitioned and placed under the supervision of two Naval Monument Specialist Officers, Lieutenants Craig Hugh Smyth and J. Hamilton Coulter.

The former Nazi Headquarters building in Munich was renamed Gallery I and used to store Göring's art collection. It's an early photograph; the camouflaged netting is gone, but the German Reich Eagle has not been removed from its perch atop the entrance. Note the barbed wire fence surrounding the building, installed early by U.S. security forces. *Courtesy National Archives.*

The required repair for the two buildings was conducted in the face of almost insurmountable difficulties, as glass and roofing materials were difficult to acquire. Barbed wire fences were constructed around the complex, along with 23 permanent guard posts manned by U.S. soldiers. All persons entering the two buildings were required to carry special passes, and all packages and handbags were examined.

By the time the first truck load of the Hermann Göring Collection arrived at the Munich Central Collection Center on July 23, 1945, an effective system for unloading, cataloguing, and storing the items had been worked out in detail. As each of the Göring objects or cases was removed from the truck, it was checked against the handwritten list prepared by Thomas Carr Howe at Unterstein. The items were then assigned an arrival number that became the property control number, as the Göring Collection was then placed in a storage room. Over the next four years the staff at the Munich Central Collection Point would repatriate most of the Göring art collection and only several of Göring's *objets d'art*.

Naval Lieutenant Craig Smyth, Head of the Munich Central Collection Point, examining items sent from the Göring Collection at Unterstein. The center painting, Vincent van Gogh's *The Bridge*, was taken from the Rothschild Collection. The painting today is in a private collection in Paris. *Courtesy National Archives.*

John Nikolas Brown, U.S. Honorary Colonel and advisor on cultural affairs (second from left), and other distinguished guests at the Munich Central Collection Center admire part of the Hermann Göring Collection. Göring's wife Emmy and daughter Edda's portrait is in the silver frame. *Courtesy National Archives.*

13

Reparations

lthough U.S. authorities at the Munich Central Collection Point returned thousands of paintings to the German occupied countries of Europe, only a few of Göring's *objets d'art* were returned. Following are two collections that were returned to France and Holland.

A silver cup and saucer from Aladdin's Cave that was returned to the Rothschild family in Paris. *Courtesy National Archives.*

Identified as a Drinking Cup (?) in the shape of a nude man on horseback by Hans Ludwig Kienle. Purchased from Eugen Gutmann and returned to Holland. *Courtesy National Archives.*

A silver, wood, and tortoise shell writing box with the accompanying utensils of ink, pen, and paper. Taken from France during World War II and returned to France on July 1, 1949. *Courtesy National Archives.*

The top of the writing box pictured above. *Courtesy National Archives.*

The history of European porcelain includes two great factories: the Saxon factory at Meissen and the Royal French manufactury at Sèvres. The beautiful Sèvres Porcelain traces its roots in French villages to the early 1700s. French King Louis XV took an intense interest in porcelain and moved the operation in 1756 to the Paris suburb of Sèvres. From the outset, the king's clear aim was to produce Sèvres Porcelain that surpassed the established Saxony works of Meissen and Dresden. The Sèvres Porcelain Factory always seemed to be in dire financial straits despite the incredibly fine works it produced. In fact, the king's insistence that only the finest items be created may have contributed to the difficulties. Only a limited number of European nobility could afford the extravagant prices demanded for such works.

King Louis XV and eventually his heir, the ill-fated Louis XVI, were obliged to invest heavily in the enterprise. Ultimately, the Sèvres Porcelain Factory produced items under the name "Royal," and thus the well known Sèvres mark was born. King Louis XV even mandated laws that severely restricted other porcelain production in France so as to retain a near monopoly for his Sèvres Porcelain. The king even willingly became chief salesman for the finest of his products, hosting an annual New Year's Day showing for French nobility in his private quarters at Versailles. He eagerly circulated among potential buyers, pitching the merits of ownership and policing the occasional light-fingered guest.

Napoleon and Josephine visited the Sèvres Factory about once a year, and the Emperor presented significant quantities of the most beautiful pieces as gifts to his accompanied foreign guests. The factory found it difficult to extract payment for these gifts. Thus, Göring was in good company with his acquisition of this royal quality porcelain.[1]

This plate and pitcher has an outer rim of lions, and in the middle of the plate is a medallion scene of gladiators fighting with a lion. *Courtesy National Archives.*

This is the medallion in the middle of the above plate. Stolen during the war from the Rothschild family by Göring, this plate and pitcher were returned to France in 1946. *Courtesy National Archives.*

This serving bowl is identical to one taken by General Maxwell Taylor, with one major flaw; this bowl has a crack across the right side. *Courtesy National Archives.*

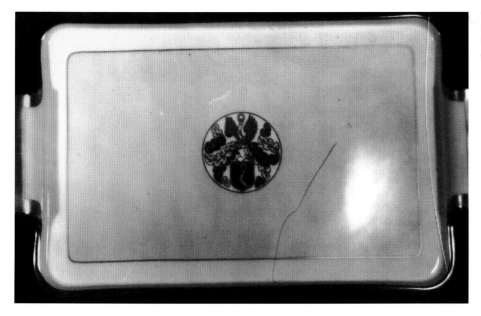

These Sèvres porcelain dishes are eleven of 163 pieces given to Göring on his 50th birthday. All the pieces were marked with Göring's coat of arms. Some of these were returned to France at a request of that country on January 21, 1948. Most of this collection was looted in Berchtesgaden while under protective custody of the U.S. Army. *Courtesy National Archives.*

A plate similar to the one on the left was auctioned for $702 on November 15, 2010, by Bonhams. The auctioned item is described as "a Sèvres porcelain dinner plate given to Reichsmarschall Herman Göring. The center contains Göring's coat-of-arms in gold, the green rim with three panels of cattle." The plate above left is identical, except it is rimed with three ermines.

Classification		Property Card Art	Mun. 5054/Berchtesgaden 16
Ceramics and glass	Subject:		Presumed Owner:
Author:	Crate containing		France
Sèvres, modern	Goerings porcelain		Sèvres
Measurements:	Material:		18. acc.to Sèvres-stamp
L W H			Inv. No.
Weight:	porcelain		Cat. No.
Depot possessor:	Arrival Condition		
Depot Cat. Goering	undamaged		
Identifying Marks:	Description		PHOTO
	23 big fruit dishes, 5 pots, 2 Salad-dishes, 1 candle-stick, 5 soup " - 1 big plate, 2 sauce " 1 fish-(?) 1 small water dish, 1 knife-rest, 1 dish with lid, 5 plates, 2 small dish, 1 spoon		
		FOR OFFICE USE: Claim No. Other Photos: Yes, No. Neg. No. 5054	
Bibliography:		File No. Movements:	

One of several Property Control Cards from the Central Munich Collection Point describing the Sèvres porcelain sent there from the Göring Collection in Berchtesgaden. *Courtesy National Archives.*

The official U.S. Army inventory compiled by Tec/4 Peck contained the following items acquired by Göring from Sèvres. It has been reported that Göring had a 2,400 piece setting of Sèvres porcelain.

11	Candleholders	10	Small Plates
9	Sugar Bowls	4	Large Serving Dishes
32	Salt Dishes, Tiny	5	Casserole Bowls
21	Knife Resters	2	Serving Dishes
7	Cake Plates, Large	8	Small Dishes
2	Flower Dishes	1	Gravy Dish
6	Sugar Bowl Spoons	12	Saucers
9	Ashtrays	1	Small Platter
4	Porcelain Tea trays	1	Gravy Dish
18	Finger Bowls		

With his insatiable desire for material possessions, Göring would require a collection this large to furnish his eight consequential Nazi establishments:

Berlin residency where Göring stored his most opulent furnishings until the deadly bombing of 1942, when he moved these valuables to Kurfuerst, the large air raid bunker near Potsdam.

Carinhall: Göring's country estate and official residence was actually a treasure trove of Beauvais tapestries, hunting scenes, and valuable paintings acquired from all over Nazi occupied Europe.

Ringewald: An eighteenth century country house used by Emmy Göring's brother. Stored here was a large, most valuable Bagatelle ceiling by Fragonard. Too large to move, it remained here and was taken by the Soviet Trophy Squad.

Gollin: A farm near Carinhall used for the storage of furniture.

Berchtesgaden: Göring's summer chalet, where he kept a small number of paintings, sculpture, and tapestries.

Veldenstein Castle: A restored sixteenth century castle where he kept some Gothic tapestries and modern German paintings.

Mauterndorf Castle: His two sisters lived here, and Göring kept some sixteenth century paintings and family ecclesiastical vestments.

Rominten Heath: A hunting lodge on 60,000 acres of land in East Prussia. The luxurious lodge was elaborately furnished, but did not contain valuable paintings.

14

Göring Objets d'art Transferred to the Bavarian Government in 1949

Then, in 1949, General Lucius D. Clay, the U.S. Military Governor of Germany, ordered the U.S. Army authorities to transfer the responsibility of the Göring Collection to the Prime Minister of the Free State of Bavaria.

In 1952, the Göring valuables were placed under the responsibility of the Federal Government in Bonn, and it was designated as trustee. Within the German Federal Foreign Office, an office was established known as the Trusteeship for the Administration of Cultural Assets, located in Munich.

At the end of 1962, the Trusteeship for the Administration of Cultural Assets declared its task complete and passed the remaining works of art on to the Ministry of the Treasury. These objects had either been legally acquired and had thus not been subject to any restitution, or were objects for which no other persons entitled to possession could be found.

In the 1960s, the best pieces were given by the Ministry of the Treasury as objects on permanent loan from the German government to German museums. Less valuable items were lent to various federal ministries or other federal government offices for purposes of decoration. Works which could not be used in this manner were sold or remained in the depot. After the Treasury Ministry was dissolved, the remaining *objets d'art* were transferred to the assets of the German Federal Ministry of Finance. Since the middle of the 1960s and even today, the German government and Bavarian state have quietly auctioned artwork acquired by Reichsmarschall Hermann Göring without providing any information on provenance for the art objects in question. Only one small statue with a missing left foot remains today in the depot of the German Federal Ministry of Finance.

A beautiful set of gold coins was designed by Professor Herbert Zeitner, who was Hermann Goring's personal jeweler. In 1939, Zeitner was the director of the master workshop for goldsmiths at the Prussian Academy of Arts in Berlin. He created vases, pitchers, goblets, bowls, crosses, tableware, and a full range of jewelry for the Göring Collection. Many of Zeitner's creations were in Berchtesgaden, and were subsequently sent to Munich by the U.S. Monuments Fine Art & Archival officers.

The box on the left is silver with precious stones, and the box on the right is silver with valuable stones and ivory. As noted in a previous photo caption, the chest on the right was not broken when recovered by U.S. Forces in Berchtesgaden. *Courtesy National Archives.*

Many of the gifts received by Göring were candle holders and candelabrums. The center of the candelabrum on the right contains a Nazi Eagle perched atop the Swastika. *Courtesy National Archives.*

The box on the left is silver with eight claw feet, and the other silver box has legs in the form of a pineapple. Jeweled boxes and chests were a focal point of Göring's collection. At Berchtesgaden 66 boxes and chests were collected. The most valuable of these chests was a big jeweled chest with ivory, gold, and stones held in gold frames representing Göring's Marshal Insignia. It was valued at 320,000 Reichsmark or a 1945 value of $128,000, which was at the time an unrealistic valuation. *Courtesy National Archives.*

This is a seventeenth century horse with a green marble base and was one of a pair. Anderson recorded two of these horses in his inventory, but with a pencil line struck through one of the entries. *Courtesy National Archives.*

These vases demonstrate the variety in Göring's collection. The right vase is engraved with relief decoration of a pine landscape in the backdrop of Mount Fuji. On the backside is a golden stylized chrysanthemum flower, the crest of the Japanese Imperial Family. Label in the bottom marked Japan. Auctioned for $2,142. The other vase decorated with an eagle was auctioned for $1,905. *Courtesy National Archives.*

This unusual wedding gift to Göring and his wife was from the town of Weissenfels, Germany. It is a silver container with three Putti angles and hinges that open and close three shells. Commissioned in 1835, it is identified as a Vexiergefäss, which is a puzzle or method of trickery to open and close a gift. *Courtesy National Archives.*

Identified as a medallion relief of a church with a coat of arms in the top center. *Courtesy National Archives.*

This gold covered bowl with valuable stones along the circumference is supported by four bears and was made by the famous firm H. J Wilm of Berlin. This was a 50th birthday gift to Göring from Mr. Wilm himself. *Courtesy National Archives.*

This beer stein is identified on the inventory card as a jug. The silver stein is covered with ivory carved hunting scenes with a bear as a knob on the silver lid.

This plated presentation plate for the Hunt Master has an engraved hunter's code: "This is the hunter's honor shield that he cherishes and preserves his game as befits the Creator in the creature's honor." The plate contains Göring's Coat of Arms at the top. Without question presentation plates, platters, and cups made up the bulk of Göring's *objets d'art*. It was auctioned for $4,762. *Courtesy National Archives.*

Silver box with sides and lid in red velvet lining, as well as ornaments with gold in Greek style adorn the box with a top covered with glass. Crafted by Zeitner, Berlin. *Courtesy National Archives.*

What makes the Zeitner collection interesting is that Göring had 20 cases of jewelry seized from the Edouard, Maurice, and Robert de Rothschild Collections. The jewelry was contained in leather cases especially designed for the individual pieces divided amongst the members of the family: Robert, Maurice, Edouard, etc. The jewelry was appraised by a representative of the Official German Gold and Art Section and was divided in two equal halves, one for Göring and the other for Adolf Hitler. A portion of this collection was delivered to Professor Herbert Zeitner. One can only surmise that the collection, which included such famous pieces as a collar containing three Giaconda diamonds, a tiara for a Hindu head piece, and an emerald collar presented by Napoleon to the Austrian Archduchess, was reworked into other valuable objects for the Reichsmarschall's collection.[1]

A gold plated facsimile of Marie's Crown as an eighteenth century desk clock with valuable stones. Auctioned for $1,071. *Courtesy National Archives.*

Misidentified in Berchtesgaden as a double goblet dated 1596, the sign of Master H. Petzolt, this item was bought from Eugen Gutmann and returned to Amsterdam June 3, 1947. The object is identified by the MFA&A inventory as a Zodiac Globe, Venetian, seventeenth century. *Courtesy National Archives.*

The Munich inventory labeled this intricate ornamental piece "a can covered with silver." *Courtesy National Archives.*

This lidded tankard, partially gilded in the Baroque style with the coat of arms of both Hermann and Emmy Göring (facing), is adorned with fruits and an eagle. On the bottom is an engraved dedication "To the wedding and the two year anniversary of the day of the appointment as Ministerpresident. The Reichsfuehrer SS as Deputy Chief and Inspector of the Prussian Secret State Police and the officials and employees of the Secret State Police Office." With the engraved signature H. Himmler and four others. Height 22 cm. Auctioned for $3,572 in 1974. *Courtesy National Archives.*

Hermann Göring was aware that the Königliche Porzellan-Manufaktur Berlin (KPM) mark stood for unique porcelain and trend-setting design at the highest level. The mark was commissioned in the autumn of 1722. The company had crafted and developed over generations and is still today in its historical location. The legendary King of Prussia, Frederick the Great, gave the company its name and symbol in 1763. The royal blue scepter is a claim to and seal of quality for each and every masterpiece of Berlin porcelain. Following are the KPM items inventoried in Berchtesgaden by U.S. Army Tec/4 Peck:

Three striking glass pieces crafted by Königliche Porzelian Manufaktur of Berlin.

This crowned bowl represents "St. George and the Dragon" from Saint Hubertus. It is partially gilt with16 semi-precious stones and consists of four separate horsemen as legs. Auctioned in 1972 for $2,857. *Courtesy National Archives.*

QUANTITY	DESCRIPTION	QUANTITY	DESCRIPTION
5	Saucers and Plates (1 piece sets)	6	Ordinary Cups
4	Large Platters	20	Small Dressing Cups
4	Large Round Platters	10	Small Saucers
3	Very Large Platters	38	Dressing Bowls
4	Large Bowls	1	Large Soup Bowl
5	Vegetable Plates	4	Medium Bowls
21	Medium Plates	1	Round Vegetable Bowl
3	Large Platters	7	Ashtrays
2	Large Round Platters	3	Round Bowls
9	Large Round Platters (different sizes)	1	Small Cream Pitcher
2	Medium Round Plates	12	Sugar Bowls with Covers
2	Small Plates	3	Sugar Bowls with Handles and Covers
1	Saucer and Plate (1 piece)	1	Pickle Dish
1	Large Tea Pot	1	Sugar Bowl Top
19	Cups	36	Medium Plates
10	Sugar Bowls with Covers	1	Small Plates
3	Cream Pitchers	1	Large Plate
1	Large Tea Pot	46	Saucers (medium)
3	Syrup Pitchers	5	Ashtrays
2	Cream Pitchers (small)	61	Pickle Dishes
3	Small Dressing Dishes	26	Dressing Saucers
1	Small Dessert Dish	46	Small Plates
47	Small Saucers	2	Saucers and Plate Sets
47	Small Cups	1	Sugar Bowl without Cover
4	Large Spoons		

Round bowl with a top; an 1850 antique with an Augsburg mark on the side and lid. Feet in the form of pine cones. In the bottom a dedication: "For the 10 April 1935, the city Augsburg." Wedding gift from the city of Augsburg. Auction $2,261. *Courtesy National Archives.*

A round bowl with a high border with reliefs of Hermann and Emmy's Coat of Arms. Dedication to their wedding on April 10, 1935. *Courtesy National Archives.*

A vessel with Göring's Coat of Arms with an eagle on the silver lid. *Courtesy National Archives.*

A teapot with Rechaud ivory handle and Rocco style relief decoration with flowers and butterflies and marked at the end of the nineteenth century. *Courtesy National Archives.*

A round plate (left) with an inside quilted mirror reflection. Marking Zeitner. *Courtesy National Archives.*

A cooler for glasses, silver with Elk stag horns on three feet, gilded Marked Zeitner, one elk head loose. *Courtesy National Archives.*

A gold plated, sterling silver tobacco can with a cover and Göring coat of arms. The front is labeled tobacco (Tabak). Marking Berlin H.J. Wilm. Auctioned for $1,190. *Courtesy National Archives.*

Two candelabrums, relief with eight sides of conical interior with five flames, engraved with Berlin bear, January 12, 1938, birthday. *Courtesy National Archives.*

Thus, the vast bulk of Hermann Göring's *objets d'art* recovered by the U.S. 101st Airborne Infantry Division were auctioned by Neumeister KG. vorm. Weinmüller on October 25, 1974; November 27, and 28, 1974; March 12 and 13, 1975; and April 23 and 24, 1975, at Brienner Strasse 14, Munich. The valuables were identified as the former property of Hermann Göring and were sold on behalf of and for the account of the Free State of Bavaria. This was at the height of the Cold War, and Bavaria was deemed in custody of Göring's valuables because at his death his homes were considered to be in Bavaria. Although Carinhall was larger and his Berlin home more plush, they were under the control of the Communists, and the trove under Western Germany control was not considered assets for the Communist governments. Today no one in Germany will discuss these Göring property auctions!

A wooden gilded Flying Angel missing its left foot. From south Germany ca 1720, purchased by Heinrich Hofer from Walter Bornheim, owner of a well-known Munich art firm. Today this sculpture is the only item of the entire Hermann Göring treasure found in the art depot of the German Federal Ministry of Finance. *Courtesy National Archives.*

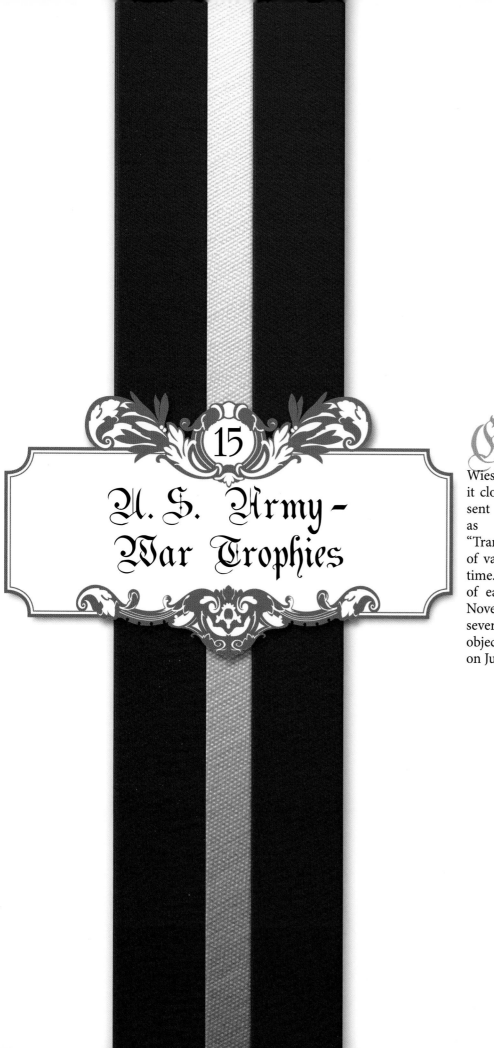

15

U. S. Army – War Trophies

Göring's Nazi-tainted objects were sent from the Munich Central Collection Point to the U.S. Wiesbaden Collection Point, and when it closed in 1950, these *objets d'art* were sent to Washington, D.C., classified as Militaristic/Nazi and stamped "Transferred to Washington." Hundreds of valuable Nazi items were sent at this time. They included a portrait painting of each of the men killed during the November 9, 1923, Munich Putsch and several of Hitler's paintings. Göring's 26 objects shipped to the Pentagon Building on June 29, 1950, were the following:

NUMBER	INVENTORY	DESCRIPTION
01	554900	Candlestick, A-jour-work with Nazi emblems for 7 candles
02	503915	Case, Ehrenbuerger document, silver
03	503926	Plate, silver gilt
04	503932	Plate, silver gilt
05	504018	Plate, silver dedication on plate
06	504613	Case for documents, silver, wood, gold, amber [Ft. Benning]
07	504621	Roll of documents, Silver on wood
08	504910	Coop for champagne, Silver *Gott mit Uns*
09	504912	Shape of a Book, silver enamel present 1938 [Ft. Benning]
10	505007	Plate, silver in middle tank
11	505025	Frame, silver Göring in frame
12	505028	Box with documents, silver copper 4 medallions
13	505506	Box, silver coat of arms Wilm 10.4.1935 [Ft Benning]
14	505526	Frame, Wood photo of Göring
15	505527	Frame, wooden photo of Hitler
16	505531	Ash tray, Silver Coat of Arms
17	505536	Cup, silver
18	505542	Cup, silver
19	505827	Box with documents, silver from March 16, 1935
20	505855	Plaquette, porcelain Goddess with wings
21	652900	Walking stick in the shape of an axe, Iron Bronze [Ft. Benning]
22	653000	Sword, Silver handle
23	653100	Sword, Iron chased
24	653200	Sword, Iron [Ft. Benning, From Mussolini]
25	653300	Sword, Steel
26	67401690	Toledo Sword, Parade Sword Göring [Gift from General Franco, Spain]
27	1579237	Colored Photo, Hermann Goring with dedications

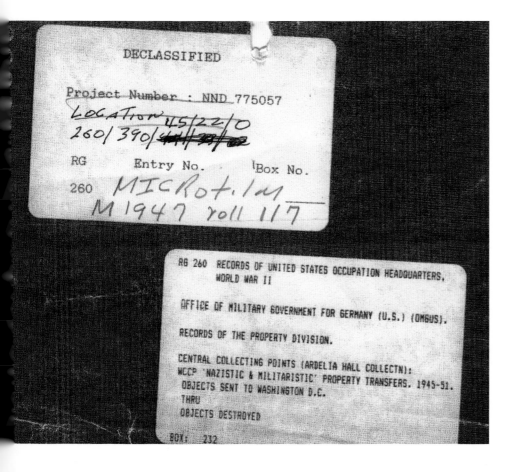

The U.S. Army Center of Military History does not have a record of the Nazi object sent to the Pentagon building in 1950. Fortunately the Munich Central Collection Point's inventory cards of this shipment are today in this box number 232 in the National Archives. These inventory cards are also available at www.fold3.com. Courtesy Kenneth D. Alford.

The silver case contains the Ehrenbuerger document (Honorable Citizen Award). It is one of several Ehrenbuerger documents presented to Göring. They were usually from a German city and signed by the mayor. *Courtesy National Archives.*

From Göring's collection, this round silver plate has an inscribed dedication etched in the center with an image of a tank. This plate is presently on display at Fort Benning, Georgia. *Courtesy Kenneth D. Alford.*

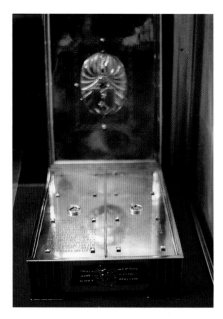

Silver and gold document case. Inside the lid is Göring's family crest and coat of arms. The case was designed to hold the important promotional documents of Göring. Today it is on display at the National Infantry Museum, Fort Benning, Georgia. *Courtesy Kenneth D. Alford.*

Author Kenneth Alford visited the U.S. Army Center of Military History on three occasions in fall 2011 and requested access to the Göring collection. To his surprise, he was advised that the Center of Military History did not have any records regarding the shipment of the Nazi-tainted objects. The Army had always been most helpful in the past, but this time he was refused access to the electronic finding aids and not allowed to view the art objects stored in their archives. From previous visits to the U.S. Army museums, the author has seen some of the above items displayed, particularly in the Infantry Museum at Fort Benning, Georgia.

Associate Counsel

During this stage of research, the Office of the Chief Attorney & Legal Services - Office of the Administrative Assistant to the Secretary of the Army became involved, and the Curator at the U.S. Center of Military History emailed:

> Right now the issue is again back with the Army legal people. I don't know what is going on here, but I am not the person to ask for additional information and I am not interested in losing my job over these matters.

As with the Göring auctions, it seems that today no one in the United States is willing to discuss Göring's acquired property. There is no question in anyone's mind that some of the above 27 valuables "walked" away from the Pentagon, and this is understandable.

This interesting silver and copper box is identified by property card 5050/28 as a box with document, engraved and containing four medallions. *Courtesy National Archives.*

This cigar chest was presented to Göring on his birthday in 1935 by the artists of the Prussian State Opera. The artists' signatures are engraved on a plate inside the top lid. The chest is today displayed at the National Infantry Museum, Fort Benning, Georgia. *Courtesy Kenneth D. Alford.*

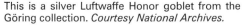

This is a silver Luftwaffe Honor goblet from the Göring collection. *Courtesy National Archives.*

Awarded To General Feldmarschall and Prussian President Hermann Göring on December 9, 1938, by the Society of 1821 for the Promotion of Industries for his innovated leadership in a non-union industry for the development of economic and military production. The silver, partly gilded, cover is shaped like a book extoling the work ethic of Göring and the German nation. This award (closed, bottom photo) is on display at the National Infantry Museum, Fort Benning, Georgia.

Courtesy National Archives.

Courtesy National Archives.   *Courtesy Kenneth D. Alford.*

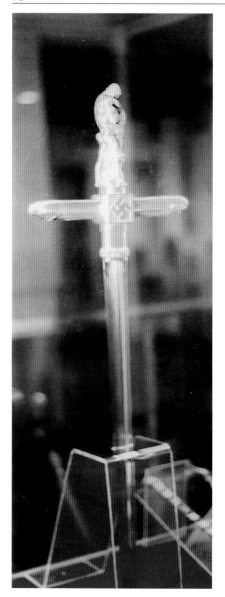

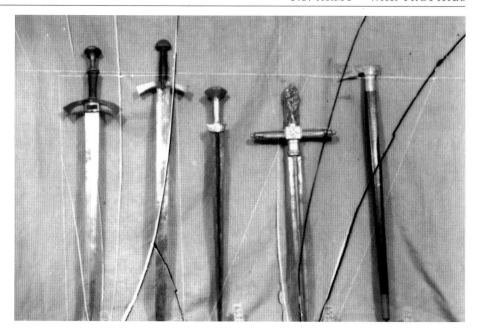

From left:
1. Sword, metal, silver handle slightly damaged
2. Sword, modern steel
3. Sword, modern, iron chased
4. Sword, modern, iron, a gift from Mussolini on Göring's 50th birthday
5. Walking stick, shaped like an ax, iron, bronze
Courtesy National Archives.

Sword number 4 above was presented to Göring by Benito Mussolini. Today on display at the National Infantry Museum, Fort Benning, Georgia. *Courtesy Kenneth D. Alford.*

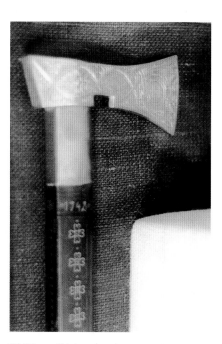

Walking Stick, number 5 above, on display at the National Infantry Museum with the caption "Walking stick, once the property of Hermann Göring, found at Berchtesgaden." Today on display at the National Infantry Museum, Fort Benning, Georgia. *Courtesy Kenneth D. Alford.*

This impressive Champaign bucket was an award from the Hitlerjugend. This gift bears the Hitler Youth emblem. The top is engraved "God is with us" and the base is imprinted S G (Sehr Geehrter – Very Respectful) General Göring. *Courtesy National Archives.*

Classification	Property Card Art	Mun. Berchtesgaden
METAL	Subject:	6740 1690
Author: Toledo, modern	"Parade-sword of marshal H.Goring"	Presumed Owner: Germany State-property ~~Ministerpräsident~~
Measurements: L W H	Material: steal, in case (wood with velvet)	Inv. No. Cat. No. Militär + Nazist
Weight: 117		
Depot possesser:	Arrival Condition	
Depot Cat.		
Identifying Marks: Artilleria F^ca Nacional de Toledo	Description	
		FOR OFFICE USE:
		Claim No.
		Other Photos: Yes, No.
		Neg. No.
Bibliography:		File No.
		Movements: 5

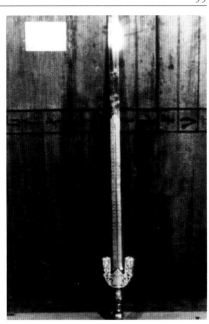

The property card with the property number 6740 and identifying mark "Artillerin Fca Nacional de Toledo" has been reclassified from ownership Ministerpresident (Head of the State of Bavaria) to Militaristic Nazist. This Toledo steel blade sword in a wooden box lined with velvet was presented to the Reichsmarschall by General Franco of Spain. A close-up of the paper next to the sword discloses the sword is property number 6089. This valuable sword is missing today.

16

The Extraordinary Blue Goose

On May 5th, C Company, 326th Airborne Engineers were in dire need of transportation, as one of their trucks was lying in a ditch beside the autobahn about 15 miles from Berchtesgaden. Sergeants Owen Henderson and Robert Smiley piled into a jeep and set out to liberate a suitable German truck. As they began to enter Berchtesgaden, they heard gunfire inside a garage. They stopped to investigate, and entering the building they found French soldiers shooting German automobiles full of holes. They spotted a sporty roadster and were warned by the French that the car was probably booby-trapped. They noticed the roadster had a starburst bullet hole in the windshield and a second shot into the left fender. The shots by the Frenchmen had not sprung a trap, so the men examined the roadster carefully. The tires were new and the gas tank full. Smiley hitched the jeep to the roadster and hauled it out onto the road. Henderson climbed cautiously behind the wheel and started the Mercedes almost immediately. The radiator leaked, but it did not take the engineers long to repair the leak. After using the car a few days the men turned it over to 101st Airborne Headquarters.

Sgt. Robert F. Mann and Lt. Robert A. McCutcheon, 506th Parachute Regiment, were driving a German truck shortly after the capture of Berchtesgaden and they turned off the main road to investigate a group of buildings. There were a few German policemen living in the buildings, but they didn't resist as the two men began to search through the buildings. In the garage they noticed a large, black, Mercedes Benz convertible touring car (Mercedes Benz Grosser 770 Offener Tourenwagon). After searching for booby traps they cleaned off the debris and started the engine. It was in perfect condition, so they drove it back and turned it over to their Commander, Captain Ronald C. Spears of the 506th Regiment, who in turn presented the car to the Division Commander, Colonel Robert F. Sink. This car was reported to have cost $35,000 and was especially built for Adolf Hitler.

These automobiles formerly belonged to Adolf Hitler (left) and Hermann Göring (right). Each was a custom built 1943 Mercedes-Benz equipped with one-quarter-inch armored plate steel and two inch bulletproof glass. The cars were captured at Berchtesgaden by members of the 101st Airborne Division. *Courtesy National Archives.*

Brigadier General Gerald J. Higgins, Assistant Division Commander, touring Southern Germany in the Mercedes formerly owned by Adolf Hitler. *Courtesy the Pratt Museum, U.S. Army.*

The Mercedes taken on May 5th by Owen and Smiley had been owned by Reichsmarschall Hermann Göring. In February 1937, Göring attended the fiftieth anniversary of the Berlin Automotive Exhibition, and during the tour spotted a Special Roadster, the Mercedes Benz 540K. He asked how long it would take to build this Special Roadster with a few modifications that included a larger 5.4-liter engine, larger fuel tank, and bullet proofing and bomb resistance.

Then Göring opened the driver's door and encountered a problem – his fat stomach pressed upon the lower portion of the steering wheel. The Director of Mercedes Benz, seeing the dilemma, discussed lengthening the driver's compartment by extending the radiator six inches. Detail specifications were drawn up, and lastly Göring requested his Special Roadster be painted Aviation Blue, in deference to his position as head of the Luftwaffe.

The windows were made of five layers of laminated glass, and the doors were reinforced with a thin sheet of steel bolted to the inside of the door panel. A steel plate was attached to the underside, and a vertical steel plate was placed behind the driver's seat, which could be raised by a hand crank.

This Special Roadster was completed in July 1937, and presented to Göring at the Mercedes Benz Agency in Berlin. Göring was ecstatic; the metallic blue was stunning. With a motorcycle escort, he test drove his new exotic toy with its supercharged engine on the autobahn and reached a speed of 100 miles per hour. Returning to the Mercedes Agency, Göring expressed to the design team that the roadster was a resounding success.

During the war years Göring's increasing weight began to cause a problem with the steering wheel, so to compensate for room for his stomach, the thickness in the driver's back cushion was reduced by four inches. This was still a problem for the gluttonous Göring; add to this his falling from favor with the Führer and lack of success in the air war, and he decided to be less flamboyant and sent the Special Roadster to Berchtesgaden, where it stayed for the rest of the war, or until taken by Sergeants Owen and Smiley.

Before long the two Mercedes, after being cleaned by their new owners, were being driven all over Berchtesgaden by members of the 101st Airborne celebrating the end of World War II. It did not take long for the higher-ups to find out about the Mercedes, and orders were issued to turn the vehicles in to the motor pool. General Maxwell Taylor spotted Göring's 540K Special Roadster and had his two star license plate placed on the roadster, now dubbed the Blue Goose by Airborne troops. In August word was received from the U.S. Treasury Department that the two prized automobiles would be a great draw for war bond rallies in the United States.

On September 10, 1945, orders were issued to ship the Special Roadster and Mercedes Tour Wagon to the United States, to be accompanied by a contingent of soldiers from the 101st Airborne Division. Although it was originally thought that both cars had belonged to Hitler, it was now determined that the Special Roadster belonged to Göring, as it sported a crest of his coat of arms on both doors. The war bond tour started on November 2, 1945, in Washington, D.C., traveling to 17 cities in the eastern part of the U.S. in 45 days.

In August 1946, the first reunion of the 101st Airborne Division was held in Indianapolis with the Blue Goose on hand. The roadster was driven on the Indianapolis Speedway, and then it was placed in storage.

The Göring Special Roadster ended up as surplus government property and was auctioned at Aberdeen Proving Grounds. On October 5, 1956, the two Mercedes Benz convertibles were sold to the highest bidder, with the Special Roadster awarded to Jacques Tunick of Greenwich, Connecticut, for $2,167. In 1958, the roadster was sold to Dr. George Bitgood of Middletown, Connecticut, who had a large collection of prewar classic automobiles. In 1998, at the age of 93, Bitgood died, and after a lengthy and costly court battle the Bitgood estate sold the Special Roadster to Carnlough International Limited of Guersey, Great Britian.

The Hermann Göring Mercedes Benz 540K Special Roadster, after considerable restoration, was returned to the condition it was in when acquired by soldiers of the 101st, to include the bullet holes in the left fender, as well as the large starburst shatter in the left window glass. Today the roadster will be recognized as a vital piece of history during which Europe was liberated in part by the blood of American troops.

The Hermann Göring Wedding Sword

17

Robert Thibodaux, Jr., was born on May 7, 1923. His residence at the time of enlistment was recorded as Vernon, Louisiana. Thibodaux was single, and his occupation was listed as a cabinet maker. Thibodaux enlisted in the U.S. Army in New Orleans on February 18, 1943. Joining the 1269th Engineer Combat Battalion in March 1944, Thibodaux had risen to the rank of staff sergeant while participating in the organization of Engineer Combat Battalions. Stationed at Camp Chaffee, he was the platoon sergeant of the 2nd platoon, Company A. Thibodaux was considered handsome and aloof, but was greatly respected by the men in Company A. Socializing was secondary to him, as preparation for the war effort was his primary mission, giving reason for his obtaining the rank of sergeant in just over one year.

On October 18, 1944, Thibodaux sailed from New York Harbor aboard the *SS Mariposa* to Marseilles, France. He fought with the 1269th until his unit reached

Sergeant Robert Thibodaux holding Göring's Wedding Sword that he had taken from Aladdin's Cave. The sword was a gift from members of the Luftwaffe when Göring married his second wife Emmy, in April 1935. The large Wedding Sword features a beautiful Damascus blade, ivory grip, and sharkskin scabbard with gold fittings. *Courtesy John R. Angolia Collection.*

Berchtesgaden. Thibodaux walked off with one of the most valuable and sought-after artifacts to emerge from World War II – the magnificent Hermann Göring Wedding Sword.

In *The Daggers and Edged Weapons of Hitler's Germany*, LTC (Ret) James P. Atwood wrote the following regarding the Wedding Sword:

> One of the most decorative swords produced during the Third Reich, this ornate piece was crafted by the firm of Carl Eickhorn and took months to complete. Herr Eickhorn informed the author that several weeks before the ceremony Field Marshal Göring learned that this sword was under production in Solingen and was to be a surprise gift for him at his forthcoming wedding. Upon hearing this, Göring made a special visit to the Eickhorn firm (in Solingen) and requested that Herr Eickhorn show him the still incomplete sword. Herr Eickhorn tactfully attempted to persuade Göring to wait until his wedding, when he was to receive the sword, but the Field Marshal would have no part of the delaying tactics. He insisted, and the weapon was produced for his inspection. Göring was extremely pleased, and requested that the scabbard be made of sharkskin dyed a royal blue to match his uniform. He then cut a small swatch of cloth from the underside of his blue Luftwaffe uniform for use as a color guide. In view of Göring's intense enthusiasm for the sword, Herr Eickhorn personally journeyed to several seaports along the North Sea coast, where he finally located a particularly fine piece of sharkskin for making the scabbard. The (blade) inscription reads, 10 April 1935 – Die Reichsluftwaffe Ihrem Oberbefehlshaber (10 April 1935, The National Air Forces to their Commander-and-Chief.)

Sergeant Robert E. Thibodaux, 2nd Platoon, claimed the Wedding Sword, and after carrying it around for a while, he sent the sword in this box to his home in Louisiana. Above is the large black box that Thibodaux used to mail the Wedding Sword. The bottom photo is the remainder of other souvenirs acquired by Thibodaux that were mailed in this box. Thibodaux used a large number of screws to close the box. His reasoning – the postal inspectors would not go to the trouble of removing all the screws to see what was inside. The box and its remaining contents were purchased by collector Thomas M. Johnson. *Courtesy of Johnson Reference Books & Militaria*

The massive sword itself was a combined effort from the finest craftsmen in Solingen. The Damascus blade required Solingen Masterswordsmith Dingler months to complete and is truly exquisite. Dingler's initials "PD" are prominently displayed in gold alongside the standard Eickhorn squirrel logo on the ricasso of the blade. In addition to the beautifully crafted blade, the second most eye-catching component of this premier weapon is the unusual pommel. The front of the Wedding Sword pommel features a representation of Göring's *Pour le Merite* (Blue Max) presented for his heroic deeds during World War I when, as an air ace, he was selected to command the elite "Flying Circus" made famous by Baron von Richthofen ("The Red Baron").

The reverse of the pommel depicts the Göring coat-of-arms: a mailed arm with a closed fist clutching a ring. The attractive hilt, which bears the *Luftwaffe* motif, was personally designed by Professor K. Dluzewski of Berlin, whose name is deeply engraved on the underside of the crossguard. The scabbard of the Wedding Sword was covered with an exquisite piece of royal blue sharkskin leather which reputedly Herr Eickhorn personally selected to match the brilliant blue color of Göring's *Luftwaffe* dress uniform (upon the suggestion of the image-conscious Hermann).

In 1953, Thibodaux sold Göring's Wedding Sword to famed collector Jim Atwood and used the proceeds to purchase a new Corvette. This unique sword is today owned by a British collector. *Courtesy of Johnson Reference Books & Militaria*

The sword was a present from the officers and men of the Luftwaffe at the time of his second marriage on April 10, 1935, to Emmy Sonnemann, a beautiful divorcee and well established actress in the State Theater.

The Wedding Sword was crated and shipped to the United States as a war trophy and proudly displayed on a den wall until tracked down by noted edged weapon author James P. Atwood, who purchased the *crème de la crème* sidearm and subsequently sold it to Mr. George R. Canaday of Anderson, Indiana. Although for obvious security reasons Mr. Canady found it necessary to store this prized artifact in a local bank vault, he kindly offered to show the former Reichsmarshall's sidearm to serious collectors if prior arrangements were made with him. The author of this section of this book did, in fact, while conducting research on one of his own earlier reference books, accept Mr. Canady's invitation and visited him at his home, photographing the Wedding Sword.

Obviously, what would be of interest to collectors and researchers world wide would be the history of the Göring Wedding Sword after its shipment from Germany to the United States by U.S. Army Sergeant Robert Thibodaux, who maintained possession of the sword until the early 1950s, when he sold it to a collector from Savannah, Georgia, LTC James P. Atwood. Whereas Thalhofer printed in his book that a figure of $6,000 was paid for the sword, Thomas M. Johnson, the author who penned this section of this book, was personally advised by Jim Atwood that the correct figure was $10,000. Thibodaux used the proceeds to purchase a new Corvette. Shortly after purchasing the Wedding Sword, Atwood was persuaded by an excellent offer to relinquish the ownership to another collector living in Anderson, Indiana, named George Canady, who owned the local bowling alley.

Canady maintained possession of the Göring sword until 1978, when the sword was consigned to a militaria auction in the United States owned by Ron Manion and named "The Foxhole." The reserve asking price in the Foxhole catalog was $60,000. The sword was subsequently purchased by Chuck Scaglione and Bob Sevier, the owners of The Cracked Pot, a militaria shop located in Buffalo, New York.

Subsequently, during the Fall of 1981 Dr. Julian Milestone, an advanced German dagger/sword collector and researcher living in Los Angeles, California, purchased the Wedding Sword from the owners of "The Cracked Pot." The sword remained in the extensive Milestone edged weapon collection until January 1984, when the sword was sold by Dr. Milestone to a private collector living in England who desires not to be named. So, in summary, this priceless work of art has changed hands only five (5) times in over sixty-five (65) years and is presently not for sale.

While conducting research on his upcoming Volume VIII of Collecting the Edged Weapons of the Third Reich, author Thomas M. Johnson (right) traveled to New Orleans on January 27, 1996. He visited SSG (Ret.) Robert Thibodaux to personally interview him about the capture and shipment of the Göring Wedding Sword to the United States. After World War II, Sergeant Thibodaux settled in his hometown of Schriever, Louisiana, and for years operated his own upholstery business. Courtesy of Johnson Reference Books & Militaria

18
Hermann Göring's Wearing Wedding Sword

LTC (Ret) James P. Atwood wrote the following regarding the Wearing Wedding Sword:

Several months after Göring received the Wedding Sword, he requested that the Eickhorn firm reproduce a facsimile sword nearly identical to the rare piece that he had received from the Luftwaffe. It was to be made of lighter metals and without a Damascus steel blade. Göring requested this second sword because the original piece was too heavy for him to wear, and he didn't wish to scratch or mar the original treasure while wearing it on formal occasions. A second Wedding Sword, much lighter in weight, was produced and given to Göring for wear. It was very similar in appearance; however, the grip was convex rather than concave.

Hermann Göring, under arrest and with his family facing execution, was moved from the underground bunker at Obersalzberg to Mauterndorf Castle, 50 miles east and away from the rapidly advancing American Army. It is incredulous that Göring would be allowed to transport several truck loads of his valuable objects, including money, liquor, and food stuffs. Indeed, he had several paintings and an unknown number of daggers that included his "wearing" Wedding Sword. To the untrained eye this was a duplicate of the wedding sword given to Göring on the occasion of his wedding by the Luftwaffe. The original sword was too heavy and pulled down the trousers of the portly Reichsmarschall. This was not an imposing way to present the second most important person in the Third Reich, so Göring had a smaller, lighter wedding sword crafted.

The sword went to Mauterndorf Castle, and then, when Göring left the castle in order to surrender to American forces and was no longer under Nazi arrest, he packed his belongings and met the American forces at Fischhorn Castle, Zell am See, south of Salzburg in Austria. Here Göring's wife and entourage remained as Göring was arrested by members of the Texas 36th Infantry Division. As he left in the early morning of May 8, 1945, he told his wife he would be away for a day or two. She would never see him free again.

The Göring staff and family stayed on the second floor of the Fischhorn while the first and third floors were used by members of the 101st, since the castle was within their occupation zone. Every day American officers came and searched all of Göring's and his staff's personal belongings, looking for weapons and information that would be of value to U.S. forces. According to Mrs. Göring, they always asked whether there were any safes hidden in the castle.

On May 15th Robert Kropp, Göring's valet since 1933, arrived with a letter from Göring that was "full of love for us but didn't mention his return." The letter also instructed Mrs. Göring to give the American officer accompanying Kropp Göring's most valuable painting, Memling's Madonna with Child. The officer and Kropp left with some of Göring's uniforms and the painting.

Although stressed by the discomforts of losing the war, Emmy Göring's personal staff remained with her, and she continued to live her normal routine of generally going to bed after two a.m. in the morning and never having breakfast before noon. She had never liked going for walks and normally remained indoors. At ten o'clock on the night of June 2nd, Mrs. Göring's good friend, Heli Bouhler, walked the stone steps to the attic of Fischhorn Castle and jumped from a window to the cobblestones, dying instantly. Her husband, Philip Bouhler, the founder of "euthanasia" of children and mentally afflicted adults, had committed suicide two weeks previously.

On June 8, 1945, Major Gene L. Brown came to Fischhorn Castle to inform Emmy Göring that all German nationals had to leave Austria. One of the officers who had been searching Göring's property in Fischhorn Castle was Major Brown, an intelligence officer for the 506th Regiment, as it was his duty to search enemy property. During one of his searches he took the "wearing" Wedding Sword of Göring for his own personal possession. Emmy then requested from Brown that she and her staff be allowed to live in their Veldenstein Castle in Neuhaus, Germany. Brown agreed and provided her with a military escort from Fischhorn Castle to Veldenstein. They left Fischhorn on June 10th. Emmy Göring had managed to hide many valuables from the searches by members of the 101st. She had in her possession half of her large jewelry collection and Göring's "Mona Lisa" of daggers. The other half of her jewelry had been stolen in Obersalzberg by her chauffeur, Kurt Hegeler. The remaining half of Mrs. Göring's jewelry would be seized by a U.S. Treasury agent within two months, and the "Mona Lisa" dagger would be stolen by Lt. Wallace L. Stephenson.

Major Brown had to have daily contact with Emmy Göring. During her many interrogations over several months, she could only recall three American soldiers' names, and they were General Dwight D. Eisenhower, General Robert L. Stack (credited with the capture of Hermann Göring), and Major Gene L. Brown. Brown returned to the United States with the "wearing" Wedding Sword. After his return to the U.S. Brown resumed his law practice in the state of Washington.

In 1980, Brown was persuaded to sell this valuable sword to the highest bidder. The "wearing" Wedding Sword was sold in June 1980. Collector Robert Thompson acquired the blade. Thompson supposedly tracked the "wearing" Wedding Sword blade back to Napoleon. The trail then goes cold for 20 years.

Lieutenant Colonel William Stewart was born in Kansas City, Missouri, on August 17, 1914. At an early age he developed an intense interest in flying airplanes. In 1937, Stewart entered the Army Air Corps and completed his basic and primary flying cadet program at Randolph and Kelly Fields, Texas, where he graduated with the rank of second lieutenant. After the Japanese attack on Pearl Harbor, Stewart was assigned to fly the C-47 cargo plane and sent to Fort Bragg, where they trained in dropping paratroopers. This was short lived, as his unit, the 62nd Troop Carrier Group, flew from Fort Bragg to Greenland, Iceland, and Scotland en route to his permanent base at Greenham Commons, 45 miles west of London.

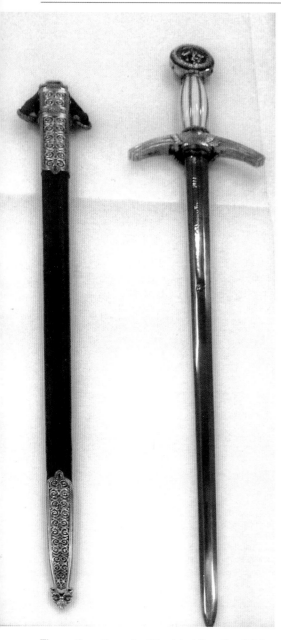

The author Kenneth Alford holding the Göring "wearing" Wedding Sword. On the left is a view of the sword and scabbard. These items are stored in a secure area within the U.S. Army Center of Military History at Ft. Belvoir, Virginia. *Courtesy Kenneth D. Alford.*

From England, Stewart's unit was assigned to Algiers in support of the 1942 North African campaign. He was Deputy Operations Officer for the 51st Air Wing and was responsible for 64 C-47 cargo planes. He would assure the planes were loaded with 3,000 pounds of supplies and schedule these planes to fly to airfields in Algiers to supply troops of Generals George Patton and Monty Montgomery. The C-47s delivered ammunition, food, and other supplies, and returned with wounded and dead soldiers. Assigned to a desk job, Stewart flew one mission, a cargo plane from Algiers to Cairo. While over the Sahara Desert he flew at 200 to 300 feet to avoid German radar.

After six months in Africa, Stewart was ordered back to the United States to organize new troop carrier groups. The return flight in a C-47 was from Algiers, across the Atlas Mountains to Liberia, then to Bathurst, Gambia. From there he flew across the South Atlantic to Ascension Island and then on to Belem, Brazil. They continued on to Florida and arrived at their final destination, Scott Field, Illinois. Within a few weeks William Stewart was assigned to be the Air Advisor to the 101st Airborne Division.

In early 1943, Stewart traveled from Scott Field to Fort Campbell, Kentucky, and reported to General William C. Lee, Commanding General of the 101st Airborne. He was permanently assigned to G-3, Operations, and provided the needed information regarding airlift requirements for training and operational combat. Additionally, he was the private pilot for General Lee. In August 1943, Stewart and Lee flew a Military Transport C-54 to London as the advance team for the transfer of the 101st to England. They were billeted in the luxurious Claridge Hotel for about two weeks prior to continuing on to Newbury and Greenham Commons, the home base of the 101st. Stewart had been stationed here at Greenham Commons the previous year, and noted the 101st Headquarters building was the same building that had been used by his old unit.

As Lee's private pilot, Stewart flew him everywhere in England, as this was Lee's preferred mode of transportation. For the trips they used a Cessna UC-78, and Lee was in the copilot's seat. After Lee's heart attack in February 1944, Stewart flew him to Prestwick, Scotland, for evacuation to the United States.

By mid-March, General Maxwell Taylor was division commander of the 101st and took over Lee's zeal for flying, as Stewart made many flights from Newberry to London and various infantry regiments of the 101st. Stewart wrote the following regarding Taylor:

> He was one of the most admirable men I've ever known and was a competitive individual. A friend of mine, Lt. Colonel Paul Danahy, the Division G-2, was an expert ping pong player. Paul would regularly beat our new general at ping pong. I mean he beat him unmercifully! It made General Taylor so mad that he threw his paddle down on the table and went up to his room two steps at a time. (It is interesting to note that Stewart wrote several pages on his and General Taylor's close friendship, but Taylor makes no mention of Stewart in his memoirs, *Swords and Plowshares*.)

For the D-Day invasion, Stewart was assigned to rear headquarters. He spent June 5th in the company of General Dwight Eisenhower and his chauffer, Kay Somersby, as they visited the troops of the 101st while they were loading into C-47s for their drop into France. Ten days later Stewart piloted the C-47 assigned to the 101st to an airstrip recently built on Omaha Beach. Stewart had little to do in Normandy, but did acquire ten Mauser 98 rifles, which he took back to England when the 101st returned.

The Division relaxed and also trained for operation Market Garden. Stewart, again with little to do, requested that he be allowed to fly into Holland as a crew member on a C-47. A friend of Stewart allowed him to copilot one of the C-47s, and after dropping the paratroopers in Holland, the crew returned to England. A few weeks later Stewart rejoined the 101st in Holland after suffering knee damage in an automobile accident. He spent a few weeks in the hospital, and as the Division was then stationed in Mourmelon, France, he purchased considerable Champaign for less that $2 a bottle.

The Bastogne affair started, and Stewart remained in Mourmelon as the Assistance Rear Base Commander. Apparently Stewart remained in Mourmelon until the 101st was approaching the Berchtesgaden area, for he writes that he caught up with the Division by flying a Cessna to a captured German airfield in Ansbach. The town had been taken two weeks previously, on April 19, 1945, by the 12th Armored Division.

From Ansbach Steward reconnected with the 101st and on into Berchtesgaden. Just south of Berchtesgaden was a building that was used for a Luftwaffe headquarters. It had several nearby chalets that were referred to as Göring's hunting lodges. Stewart was assigned one of these chalets that had been occupied by German General Bruno Loerzer. The General and World War I Ace had left in a hurry, and Stewart used Loerzer's desk, office, bedroom with twin beds, oil paintings, and Persian rugs. Elsa Kriber, the housekeeper and Loerzer's aunt, still occupied the building.

According to Stewart, Kriber gave him several medals that had been presented to German officers, including the Order of the Crown of Italy, and many of Göring's personal items. Stewart returned to the Unites States with some great souvenirs. He was then assigned to the 82nd Airborne Division at Fort Bragg in his continuation of a 30-year career with the Air Force. To Stewart's credit he wrote, "I was never in the rough stuff."

On July 20, 1954, William Stewart loaned the Washington State Historical Society some of the souvenirs he had acquired during World War II. His connection with the State of Washington began in 1938 while he was stationed

Photographs can tell a story, a sad one in this case. In the summer of 1945, Lt. Col. William Stewart poses proudly wearing Göring's coat and hat, holding SS General Bruno Loerzer's sword, and displaying Göring's large silk underwear. Göring's boots are in the background. The original owner of the hat and coat, Göring received a death sentence for war crimes, a later owner died homeless in California, and then a collector had the items seized by the U.S. Marshall Service in a drug bust. Thomas Wittmann, who acquired the boots, borrowed money from a bank for the purchase and his wife divorced him for wasting their money on Third Reich memorabilia. With a sense of humor he wrote: "My first wife hated these things and the hobby in general. She could never understand why buying a Chained-SS dagger was more important than taking the family to Disney World." *Courtesy of Pratt Museum, United States Army.*

at Fort Lewis. It was here that he met a Tacoma girl, Marjean, whom he married in February 1939. He loaned the Society Hermann Göring's top coat, hat, boots, ties, underwear, etc. He also loaned them five folios containing lithographs brush etched in black and white. On April 1, 1958, Colonel Stewart, now stationed at Maxwell Air Force Base in Alabama, requested the Washington State Historical Society to send the Göring items on loan to the 101st Airborne Museum in Fort Campbell, Kentucky. The museum at Fort Lewis requested that the Göring uniform be on display at their newly established museum prior to shipment to Fort Campbell. Stewart agreed with the Fort Lewis request and wrote that he would notify the Curator at Fort Campbell to expect the material in August.

Twenty years later, after finding out the Göring collection had not been received at the military museum in Fort Campbell, Frank D. Gish, a military collector, telephoned the Washington State Historical Society and inquired about the status of the Göring collection. After a frantic search Kenn Johnson, a Society staff member, found a crated box in the boiler room with the address of the 101st Museum in Fort Campbell. At the request of a member of the Society the box had been built, and a carpenter had been instructed to "mail it out." In the forgotten box was a pair of light brown jack boots, low black-leather dress boots, a cap complete with Nazi insignia, a leather aviator's helmet, a field-gray greatcoat, two handkerchiefs, a pair of knee-high silk elastic stockings, two cravats (dress string ties), some silk underwear (size 48), an autographed portrait of Göring, and five bound folios of art. The handkerchiefs and underwear contained the monogram "H. G." The portrait was dated 1934. A few days later Gish telephoned the Society that the museum that was to be the destination of the Göring collection had burned down "some time ago." This was not true and was a form of deception, as Gish worked an angle to get his hands on the collection.

A few days later on February 26, 1979, in Stewart's home in San Bernardino, California, Colonel William Stewart signed a "To Whom It May Concern" that authorized Mr. Frank D. Gish as his representative in searching and taking immediate possession of the following items:

> Hermann Göring's Reichsmarschall Dress Hat
> Reichsmarschall Top Coat
> Matching Reichsmarschall Trousers
> Patent Shoes with spurs attached
> Brown Dress Boots
> Flying helmet
> Misc. (socks, snap-on tie, and shorts)
> Five Folios containing lithographs, etchings brushed in black and white.

On March 24, 1979, Stewart signed a receipt for the above items, receiving them from his agent Frank D. Gish.

The above items were purchased from Stewart by the Texas collector team of Ben Swearingen and Ben Curtis; Gish had a role in this deal and probably received a commission. Over the years Swearingen and Curtis sold all of these relics, with Göring's military hat and grey field coat going to Phil Johnson, who later died as a homeless street person in California.

Göring's wearing Wedding Sword, which had been previously taken by Major Gene L. Brown and subsequently sold to Robert Thompson, and Göring's military hat and field coat, all taken as souvenirs from Berchtesgaden, were reunited when these items were purchased by Wolfe-Hardin, Finest Quality Antiques, Long Beach, California.

Laguna Beach is about thirty miles south of Long Beach and home to Brynn Garrett Downey, then a 45-year-old mortgage broker. From 1993 to 1996 Downey sold $7 million dollars worth (more than nine tons) of marijuana for the Mexican drug cartel headed by kingpin Angel Rios. Downey used $2 million of the profit from this venture to purchase Nazi memorabilia, including Field Marshall Hermann Göring's Luftwaffe coat, hat, and personal wearing Wedding Sword.

Arrested by Federal drug agents in 1997, Downey pleaded guilty to one count of conspiracy to distribute marijuana and three counts of filing false tax returns. Facing a 10 year prison sentence, Downey cooperated with the Federal investigators, and he paid the Internal Revenue Service $500,000. His Nazi memorabilia collection was seized by the U.S. Marshal Service. Downey was then sentenced to 30 months in prison.

Downey's Nazi collection, consisting of 49 expensive items (see appendix B), was seized by the U.S. Drug Enforcement Agency on May 29, 1997. A year later the items were placed in the custody of the United States Marshals Service, which quickly had the valuables appraised from photographs by a Smithsonian appraiser who had a background in the collection of Third Reich memorabilia. It is interesting to note the wearing Wedding Sword had an invoice value of $2 million and was downgraded by the Smithsonian appraiser to $250,000. Göring's coat and hat were reevaluated downward from $250,000 to $50,000.

Per Federal regulations, the seized Nazi material could have been auctioned to the highest bidder, with the proceeds to be used in the continuing battle against drugs. But the U.S. Army Center of Military History showed an interest in these items and, according to Federal Regulations:

3. Other Department Components

If no investigative bureau chooses to place the property into official use and the property had not been equitably transferred, other Department components may, by written request to Director, U.S. Marshals Service, seek transfer of the forfeited property for its official use.

Taking advantage of the ruling of Other Department Components, the Center of Military History requested the property. The request was approved, and in February 1999, the U.S. Marshals Service was asking, "Do you know if someone will be picking the Nazi property up shortly?" On August 10, 1999, Göring's "wearing" Wedding Sword, coat, hat, and the remaining military memorabilia were transferred to the Center of Military History by the Asset Forfeiture and Money Laundering Section. The Marshals Service requested to be reimbursed for expenses in the amount of $1,429.41 from Bluechip Storage & Transportation.

It took six months for this valuable collection to arrive at the U.S. Army Center of Military History at Fort McNair, Washington, D.C., during February 2000. Even longer, after persistent pestering from the U.S. Marshals Service, on March 15, 2001, the Center of Military History sent them a handwritten check for $1,429.41. For this amount of money the U.S. Army received a collection worth several million dollars. Too bad this Nazi collection is now hidden from public view.

Most of the Hermann Göring Collection of *objets d'art* acquired by the U.S. Army and sent to Washington, D.C., from Germay in 1952, are not on display and are unaccounted for. Many of these valuables "walked away" from their storage facility in the Pentagon. The seizure of Göring's items by U.S. soldiers was not appropriate, but maybe looting, in this one case, is not an ugly word, along with the pestilence and misery that has always followed conquerors' armies in the aftermath of wars. These fragments that followed the victors home were not swallowed up by a bureaucratic government, nor did they become meaningless exhibits in European castles or museums. They have given great enjoyment to collectors the world over.

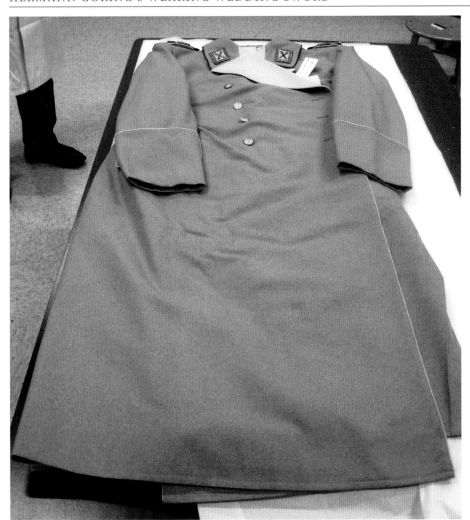

Reichsmarschall Hermann Göring's coat and hat seized by the U.S. Marshall Service during a drug bust. These objects are today property of the U.S. Army. They were originally taken as war booty during 1945 by Lt. Col. William R. Stewart. *Courtesy Kenneth D. Alford*

A

APPENDIX

Inventory of
Gold and Silver Items
in Göring's Collection

No	Qty	OBJECT	DESCRIPTION
1		1 Floor room,	33 rugs of different sizes
2		1 Tapestry	1st floor room - 99 - all sizes & ages
3		1st Floor	hall/rug 40 x 60 ft.
4	2	Antique chests -	wood & bronze, antique Value ???
5	1	Ash tray - silver	gold coated.835 fine, coat-of-arms of Goering
6	1	Ash tray - silver:	gold coated, gift of the Ministry of Commerce
7	1	Ash tray & cigar holder:	silver, .800 fine, with figures, gift of City of WeisBranfels
8	1	Ashtray silver -	.835 fine, made by Zeitner
9	2	Basins -	silver, gold plated, base with big quartz and topaz stones decorated
10	1	Basket - silver	coat-of-arms, antique
11	1	Basket - silver	hand saw-d .925 fine
12	1	Basquet (basket)	silver .800 fine, given by Schulg 1938
13	1	Basquet (basket) -	silver, gold coated - .835 fine, fruit basquet (basket), base decorated with stones
14	1	Basquet (basket) -	silver, gold coated; base with stones decorated (damaged-several stones missing), .835 fine, Zeitner, Berlin
15	2	Basquet (baskets) -	silver, gold coated, .835 fine, made by Zeitner, Berlin
16	1	Baton Marshall - silver	Herman Goerings
17	1	Book - silver:	silver, signature book of H. Goering
18	1	Bottle - Perfume	Crystal and silver
19	2	Bottles	silver bases
20	1	Bowl -	quartz, silver base: silver base, decorated with sapphires & pearls
21	1	Bowl -	silver base, agate, Zeitner, Berlin, .925 fine
22	1	Bowl -	silver, gold coated
23	1	Bowl -	silver, gold coated, .830 fine, Zeitner, Berlin
24	1	Bowl -	silver, gold coated, base damaged, stone decorated (amethysts)
25	1	Bowl -	silver, gold coated, base decorated with half gems
26	1	Bowl -	silver, gold coated, base with topaz & smoked quartz stones (damaged)
27	1	Bowl -	silver, gold decorated, made (he did not finish)
28	1	Bowl -	vase (wine cooler) with topaz stones, .835 fine, gold coated.
29	1	Bowl - Lapis	lazuli stone: half gem, made of acliate stone? R.M.
30	1	Bowl - quart	silver base decorated with cloisonne stones
31	1	Bowl - quartz stone	big bowl with sapphires, silver base
32	1	Bowl - quartz stone	silver base with aquamarine stones & pearls
33	1	Bowl - silver	gold coated amber & half gems, made by Wrlen, Berlin
34	1	Bowl - silver,	gold coated

No	Qty	OBJECT	DESCRIPTION
35	1	Bowl - silver,	gold coated: base decorated with amethysts and angels playing musical instruments, gift of Goering's daughter Edda
36	1	Bowl & cover	silver .855 fine - not engraved gold coated
37	1	Bowl Crystal	silver cover has signature of Hitler
38	2	Bowl silver	legs, handles
39	1	Bowl silver -	engraved, gift from the Goering works to Goering
40	1	Bowl silver-	baroque style, .800 fine
41	1	Bowl silver-	coat-of-arms of H. Goering, .925 fine
42	1	Bowl silver-	pedestal, silver smith art
43	1	Bowl- silver	.835 fine, made by Zeitner, Berlin, engraved gold Coated
44	1	Bowl- silver	.925 fine, christening bowl with engraved scenes of the - gold Coated
45	1	Bowl- silver	legs bear figures; .925 fine, 16 stones, amethyst; with plate
46	1	Bowl silver -	Chinese or Japanese make
47	1	Bowl silver -	cover damaged, four pieces of half gems missing
48	1	Bowl silver -	engraved with Goerings (coat-of-arms) Value
49	1	Bowl silver -	fruit, not engraved ???
50	1	Bowl silver -	gift from the Prussian Ministry
51	1	Bowl silver -	made of silver coins - Gift of the City of Augsburg
52	1	Bowl silver -	marked KDDK & coat-of-arms of Goering
53	1	Bowl silver:	Chinese or Japanese, silver smith art, high art value - gold Coated
54	1	Bowl- silver:	silver legs, .800 fine, not engraved
55	3	Bowls -	candle holders, silver, gold coated: base with amethyst stones
56	1	Box	ivory and silver, silver base, damaged cover
57	1	Box	#NAME?
58	1	Box -	Ivory & silver: cover bears picture of Diana
59	1	Box -	silver, gold coated antique, hand worked
60	1	Box -	silver, .925 fine and half gems: Prussian Eagle box decorated with stones
61	1	Box -	silver, .925 fine: chest, silver smith art
62	1	Box -	silver, .925 fine: com. (commemorative - my insert) of all Pour de Merit Holders of World War #1
63	1	Box -	silver, .925 fine: com. (Commerative, ie my insert), box of the German Art Society 1934
64	1	Box -	silver, gold coated
65	1	Box -	silver, gold coated, with big aquamarine stone
66	1	Box -	silver, gold coated, with pheasant scene
67	1	Box -	silver, with half gems
68	1	Box - gold & silver:	acliate foundation with decorations of Nazi insignias

No	Qty	OBJECT	DESCRIPTION
69	1	Box - Ivory and silver;	base decorated with stones and pearls
70	1	Box - Jewel	gold and silver gift from the City of Berlin to Goering 1937; box is decorated with half gems & cameos (Damaged)
71	1	Box - Jewel	silver & gold plated decorated with Goering's Marshal insignia
72	1	Box - Jewel	silver, .925 fine
73	1	Box - Jewel	silver: big antique jewel box with lapis lazuli decorations ???
74	1	Box - Jewel	silver: damaged cover
75	1	Box - Jewel gold & silver:	gold & silver malachite decorated, jewel box with gold figures, decorated sides, pearls
76	1	Box - silver & gold:	gold eagle, Goering's coat of arms inside, gift of the SA to Goering
77	1	Box - silver,	gold coated - antique
78	1	Box - silver, gold coated:	.925 fine, tobacco box, Zeitner, coat-of-arms - Goering
79	1	Box - silver, gold coated:	cover with large smoke topaz, hunting scenes
80	1	Box - silver, gold coated:	.925 fine - gift of Senate of the City of Hamburg
81	1	Box - silver:	gift of the German Labor Service
82	1	Box - silver:	Air Force insignia & coat of arms H.G.
83	1	Box - silver:	gift of the City of Fuerth
84	1	Box of fine silver	approx. 15 lbs
85	1	Bronze bowl -	antique
86	1	Bronze candle holder	
87	2	Bronze Candlesticks:	bronze art
88	1	Bronze Watch -	antique, made in Paris ???
89	1	Buffalo -	silver, gold coated with cryolite stones
90	1	Bust, silver & bronze:	head of girl in bronze, head decoration silver with stones
91	1	Butter knife	
92	1	Butter knife silver,	.925 fine, gold coated
93	8	Butter knifes - silver	
94	2	Candelabrums	silver - five arms
95	2	Candelabrums	silver - five arms, .925 fine
96	2	Candelabrums	silver - wire arms
97	10	Candelabrums	silver, .830 fine
98	1	Candelabrums	silver, baroque style
99	2	candelabrums	silver, gold coated, 5 arms
100	1	Candelabrums	Tin
101	2	Candelabrums - 5 candles,	silver, gold coated
102	2	Candelabrums- silver,	four arms RM.
103	2	Candle holder -	bronze
104	1	Candle holder - silver,	gold coated

No	Qty	OBJECT	DESCRIPTION
105	1	Candle holder - silver:	.950 fine, made in Koln
106	1	Candle stick -	silver, gold coated - damaged
107	1	Champaign cooler ,	silver - gold coated
108	1	Chest -	Malachite, watch-holder
109	1	Chest -	silver with amber decorations "Meine Falken"
110	1	Chest -	silver, gold coated jewel chest with bronze claws, cover made of Nephrite* and other half gems, engraved with Goering's coat-of-arms
111	1	Chest -	silver, gold coated, made by Zeitner, containing Egyptian gold decorations - antique
112	1	Chest -	silver, gold coated, scene of farm engraved on cover, Goering's coat-of-arms
113	1	Chest - floor;	gold coated with Goering's coat-of-arms in rubies and smaragts
114	1	Chest - Jeweled	ivory, gold, silver: big jewel chest (damaged) with stones, silver box, gold decorations, stones held in gold frames (Goering's Marshal insignia)
115	1	Chest - silver	gold Coated coat of arms of Goering with rubies
116	1	Chest - silver,	gold coated, decorated with army-life scenes and swastika eagle
117	1	Chest - wood:	lapis lazuli stones, decorated - antique, Toledo made? (His question mark) ???
118	1	Cigar box	gold coated box from Karlsruhe
119	1	Cigar box -	silver
120	1	Cigar Box -	silver, gold coated
121	1	Cigar Clipper -	silver - Goering's form of an eagle claw
122	1	Clock -	Bronze: old clock
123	1	Clock	silver and gold coated, Parisian make
124	1	Coffee & Tea Service	silver consisting of 3 kettles (1 tea, 1 coffee, 1 san
125	1	Coffee pitcher - silver:	.835 fine, with engraved coat-of-arms of H. Goering, made by Schrader, Berlin
126	1	Cream Bowl - silver	not engraved
127	1	Cream Can - silver:	1829 with coat-of-arms
128	1	Cream spoon	
129	1	Cup -	gold and silver - antique, stones, age ?? Price
130	1	Cup -	silver - with amethyst stones
131	1	Cup -	silver, antique silver smith art, (Nürnberg) est. val.
132	1	Cup -	silver, gold coated
133	1	Cup -	silver, gold coated - base with rubies
134	1	Cup -	silver, gold coated, .800 fine, antique with scenes of a hunt
135	1	Cup -	silver, gold coated, .835 fine
136	1	Cup -	silver, gold coated, antique with ball feet

No	Qty	OBJECT	DESCRIPTION
137	1	Cup -	silver, gold coated: .835 fine, Zenner, Berlin, not engraved
138	1	Cup -	silver, gold coated: Florentine auto
139	1	Cup -	silver, gold coated: Florentine cup, antique (Florence)
140	1	cup - quartz,	silver base: silver base (gold. coated); contains stones
141	1	cup - quartz,	silver base: silver base, gold coated; contains stones cloisonne
142	1	Cup - silver	Heavy gold Coated stones, (turquoise, aquamarine, etc.)
143	1	Cup - silver -	.800 fine, hunting trophy 1936
144	1	Cup - silver -	engraved: "Life starts at 50", .800 fine
145	1	Cup - silver,	gold coated- no cover
146	1	Cup - silver, gold coated:	.835 fine, Zeitner, Berlin; decorated with half gems
147	1	Cup - silver, gold coated:	antique
148	1	Cup - silver, gold coated:	base with cryolite stones
149	1	Cup - silver, gold coated:	decorated with amethyst stones
150	1	Cup - silver, gold coated:	.835 fine, Zeitner, Berlin with (he did not finish)
151	1	Cup - silver, gold coated:	3 bone rings on base - made by Wrlen, Berlin
152	1	Cup - silver, gold coated:	base with cryolite stones
153	1	Cup - silver, gold coated:	ivory carvings, antique
154	1	Cup - silver, gold coated:	made by Zeitner, Berlin, bison relief pictures
155	1	Cup - silver, gold plated:	.835 fine, Zeitner, Berlin
156	1	Cup - silver:	12 lotig = .800 fine
157	1	Cup - silver:	antique with scenes, antique
158	1	Cup - silver:	antique, 13 lotig, hand made
159	1	Cup - silver:	coat-of-arms of H. Goering
160	1	Cup - silver:	coat-of-arms, .835 fine
161	1	Cup - silver:	engraved "KH"
162	1	Cup - silver:	Goering's trophy for air victories, 1939,.835 fine
163	1	Cup - silver:	gold plated
164	1	Cup - silver:	inside gold plated
165	1	Cup - silver:	marked: Edda
166	1	Cup - silver:	.835 fine, made by Zeitner, Berlin - not engraved
167	1	Cup - silver:	.925 fine, made by Zeitner, Berlin, hunting trophy with swastika and inscription
168	1	Cup - silver:	.925 fine, with elk head
169	1	Cup - silver:	.925 fine, Xmas present of Berlin Children to Goering
170	1	Cup - silver:	antique
171	1	Cup - silver:	antique, engraved "Guidon fock" 1688, inside gold plated
172	1	Cup - silver:	engraved with swastika
173	1	Cup - silver:	Gift of the German Police to Goering

No	Qty	OBJECT	DESCRIPTION
174	1	Cup - silver:	gold plated
175	1	Cup - silver:	Mass cup, eight
176	1	Cup - silver:	.925 fine with engraved coat-of-arms of H. Goering
177	1	Cup - tin, gold coated:	antique
178	1	Cup - Trophy, silver:	Donation to Goering by Steel Helmet Organization, cost-of-arms of Goering
179	1	Cup (china) and saucer -	antique- Value ???
180	1	Cup silver -	big trophy cup with engraved coat-of-arms given by the air force to Goering
181	1	Cup silver -	decorated with stones given from Frick to Goering
182	1	Cup silver -	donation of Himmler to Goering
183	1	Cup silver -	hunting cup, antique
184	1	Cup silver -	Old silver smith art with figures, excellent work
185	1	Cup silver - inscription:	To the victor in aerial combat
186	1	Cup silver and gold	With deer head .835 fine, Zeitner, Berlin
187	1	Cup, silver -	big Cup silver; gift of the German Sea Fishing Industry - Goering
188	4	Cups -	beakers, silver with eagles & H. Goering coat-of-arms
189	3	Cups -	silver - not engraved
190	10	Cups -	silver (gold plated) R.M.
191	9	Cups -	silver, gold plated: Goering coat-of-arms, .835 fine
192	2	Cups -	silver: base decorated with half gems (blue turquoise?)
193	2	Cups - Bronze:	vietal art work
194	25	Cups - silver, gold coated:	Hubertus coated cups, .925 fine, 1935
195	2	Cups - silver, gold coated:	Zeitner, moose & deer pictures
196	2	Cups - silver:	antique 1596, gold coated
197	2	Cups - silver:	engraved with proverbs, .900 fine
198	9	Cups silver:	.925 fine with Goering's coat-of-arms engraving
199	8	Cups silvers	silver, .835 fine, not engraved
200	10	Cups silvers	silver, .925 fine, not engraved
201	36	Cups silvers -	engraved with coat-of-arms of H. Goering
202	3	Cups, - silver:	gold coated, engraved, .835 fine, Zeitner, Berlin
203	1	Deer -	silver, gold coated, with cryolite* stones
204	1	Deer - silver,	gold plated: silver smith art with half gems
205	1	Desk Assembly -	silver: box & 3 desk assembly
206	1	Drinking Cup silver	silver coin on cover, hand worked silver smith art
207	4	Figures silver, gold plated:	maidens, decorated with half gems
208	1	Finder Bowl -	silver - not engraved
209	1	Fish Tray - silver	donation to Goering from the German Fishing Industry
210	2	Flower Vases - silver	Japanese make
211	1	Fork	silver gold coated, .925 fine

No	Qty	OBJECT	DESCRIPTION
212	1	Fork	.925 fine, silver, gold coated
213	1	Fork silver,	.925 fine, gold coated
214	3	Forks - silver,	big, gold coated
215	9	Forks - silver,	engraved, antique
216	4	Forks - silver,	gold coated, small, .925 fine
217	2	Forks, 2 spoons -	silver, gold coated
218	1	Fruit basket,	silver - fruit basket with deer & figure
219	1	Fruit Bowl -	silver
220	1	Fruit Bowl - silver	not engraved
221	1	Fruit plate	silver, ornamented with coat-of-arms - Goering
222	1	Holy Mary & child - ivory:	antique Value ???
223	1	Honor book -	silver, gold coated: gift of the Chamber of Commerce (no gold plaque containing!)
224	1	Horn - plastic and silver	damaged ???
225	1	Horse - Bronze:	marble foundation
226	1	Jar -	glass & silver: coat of arms of Goering
227	1	Jar - quartz & silver frame:	cloisonne stones
228	1	Jar - silver:	.925 fine, with half gems & amber? (My mark) made by Wrlen, Berlin, damaged
229	7	knifes	silver gold coated, .925 fine, coat of arms of Goering
230	19	Large Finger Bowls	silver - Chinese make
231	2	Large spoons	.925 fine, silver, gold coated
232	1	Light Stand - silver:	.835 fine, big floor lamp
233	1	Light stand decoration -	silver, gold coated with string of 4 busts of ladies, with stone decoration, badly damaged
234	1	Liquor glass & cup holder -	silver, gold coated (little cups missing)
235	1	Liquor Set - silver	consisting of: 6 silver liquor cups & chest with coat-of-arms of Goering
236	1	Map - silver:	containing Reich Defense Law of 1935
237	1	Match Box	silver, gold coated, scenes of deers, made (he did not finish)
238	1	Mirror -	silver, gold coated: with gem stones decorated
239	1	Photo Frame -	silver, Goerings
240	1	Pick Ax -	for mountain climbing - silver Value ???
241	1	Picture -	silver and ivory with silver, gold coated chain, picture animal agate stones ???
242	1	Picture frame -	silver, gold plated ---
243	1	Picture frame:	silver, gold coated; Goering's wife and child lapis-lazuli (6001) Library of Congress
244	1	Pitcher -	brass only
245	1	Pitcher - silver:	.800 fine
246	1	Pitcher - silver:	ivory handle

No	Qty	OBJECT	DESCRIPTION
247	1	Pitcher - silver:	.800 fine with cover of ivory
248	1	Pitcher - silver:	.800 fine, Klon Kosch, Wien
249	1	Plaque - silver	representing coat of arms of a city, antique
250	1	Plaque of silver:	from the German Society in Stockholm
251	1	Plate -	silver, gold coated with cloisonne stones; scene of St. Hubertus and the bear, Zeitner, Berlin
252	1	Plate -	silver, gold coated, .800 fine
253	1	Plate - silver	antique silver smith art. hand worked scenes in silver
254	1	Plate - silver -	hand worked silver
255	1	Plate - silver and	mother of pearls: antique, est. value?? (his question mark)
256	1	Plate - silver,	gold coated: big plate with stone decorated border, air force eagle engraved (MINE)
257	1	Plate - silver,	gold coated; simple silver plate
258	1	Plate - silver, gold coated:	.830 fine, made by Zeitner, decorated with 4 girl busts
259	1	Plate - silver, gold coated:	antique, not engraved
260	1	Plate - silver, gold coated:	engraved, cow, first production of synthetic butter, 1942
261	1	Plate - silver, gold coated:	made by Zeitner, Berlin, .835 fine, engraved with Mother & child
262	1	Plate - silver, gold coated:	with designs, .925 fine, engraved
263	1	Plate - silver:	Donation from the air raid wardens of Germany to Goering
264	1	Plate - silver:	fish plate given by the aero club
265	1	Plate - silver:	gold plated: not engraved, heavy gold coat
266	1	Plate - silver:	.800 fine silver plate, donation of the Mark Brandenburg to H. Goering
267	1	Plate - silver:	.800 fine, made by Linkosch, Wien
268	1	Plate - silver:	.830 fine with dec, borders
269	1	Plate - silver:	antique engraved pictures of Knights at tournament
270	1	Plate - silver:	antique, worked border edges
271	1	Plate - silver:	Donation of the City of Hall
272	1	Plate - silver:	Donation of the Herman Goering Division
273	1	Plate - silver:	gold plated: eagle missing

No	Qty	OBJECT	DESCRIPTION
274	1	Plate - silver:	hunting trophy, .925 fine, with ruled picture of hunt
275	1	Plate - silver:	not engraved, .925 fine
276	1	Plate - silver:	Prussian Eagle with amber inlaid
277	1	Plate - silver:	renaissance style
278	1	Plate - silver:	Spanish, hand worked, silver smith art
279	1	Plate silver -	Donation (engraved) to Goering (Coat-of-arms)
280	1	Plate silver	
281	2	Plates -	silver, gold coated, .800 fine
282	2	Plates - silver, gold coated:	engraved with dates of February's rearmament in the air
283	6	Plates - silver-gold coated:	.925 fine, engraved
284	3	Plates silver-	donation of the Workers Union to Goering
285	5	Plates silver-	hand wrought silver, engraved
286	64	Plates silver-	of various designs
287	5	Plates silver-	with coat-of-arms of H. Goering, .835 fine
288	1	Platter -	silver, gold coated with eagles, eagle claws feet, cryolite stones
289	1	Platter - silver:	.800 fine
290	1	Platter - silver:	antique, hand made scenes of Paucus
291	1	Pot -	Tin
292	1	Roman art -	wagon with lions, group of five Value ???
293	1	Safe box:	Old Bronze antique Value ???
294	1	Saucer - silver	Coat-of-arms - Goerings
295	1	Scroll Container - silver	Sch--cidsmiths
296	1	Scroll holder - silver	Nephrite stone & engraved stones
297	1	Sealing Box -	tin, with coat-of-arms of Herman Goering (Stone lapis lazuli)
298	1	Service -	silver, gold coated, consisting of 8 pieces
299	1	Service spoon	silver gold coated, .925 fine
300	1	Service spoon - .	.925 fine, gold coated
301	1	Set Children silver -	consisting of 4 pieces
302	8	Set of Chandeliers:	silver, gold coated and quartz stones, decorated base with gems

No	Qty	OBJECT	DESCRIPTION
303	1	Set of cookie forms	silver H.G. coat-of-arms, one form missing
304	1	Set of liquor glasses -	quartz and silver: silver, gold coated with gem decorated base
305	1	Set of silver (table):	4 pieces: fork, knife, spoon, sugar spoon (gold coated)
306	1	Shoe Lacer - silver	
307	1	Shrine -	bronze and silver - antique shrine, decorated with lapis lazuli stones
308	1	Soup Tray & Bowl -	spoon & tray & bowl
309	1	Spatula -	.925 fine, gold coated
310	3	Spoons	silver, gold coated .925 fine
311	6	Spoons - silver	engraved, antique
312	1	Statue of Monteiro	- with gem stones, antique Value ???
313	1	Statute	The Holy Michael, silver with gem stones, antique Value ???
314	1	Statute - silver:	girl figure, silver, gold coated
315	1	Statute of Neptune:	silver, antique Value ???
316	1	Statute, Bronze	Woman Value ???
317	1	Sugar Box - silver	old silver
318	1	Sword - steel:	Spanish sword ? Antique s ???
319	7	Swords	(1 Toledo, 1 Italian) antique value ----
320	1	Table Bell - silver	
321	1	Tea Cup -	not engraved, .830 fine
322	1	Tea Cup - pitcher:	silver, engraved Donation by D. V. Lammers
323	1	Tea Cup - silver:	engraved (donation from children)
324	1	Tea Kettle - silver:	cover
325	1	Tea or Coffee Pitcher -	silver: engraved with coat-of-arms of H. Goering, .925 fine
326	1	Tea Pot - silver	with mahogany handle
327	1	Teapot - silver:	silver work
328	2	Teapots - baroque -	silver: antique silver baroque
329	2	Teapots - silver:	ivory handles & cover, .900 fine
330	1	TinPlate-	1741

No	Qty	OBJECT	DESCRIPTION
331	1	Tray - silver, gold coated:	antique
332	1	Tray - silver, gold coated:	coat-of-arms of H. Goering
333	1	Tray - silver, gold coated:	engraved, donation from the German Hunting Association
334	5	Trays - with designs,	antique
335	1	Tureen - silver	consisting of tray & cover
336	1	Vase -	silver and mother-of-pearl; antique with stones heavily damaged
337	1	Vase - silver, gold coated	.835 fine, made by Zeitner, Berlin
338	1	wall picture - silver	antique - can not be evaluated ???
339	1	Wine cooler -	silver, gold coated: big vase
340	1	Writing & desk set -	silver, gold plated: clock, 2 boxes with jades
341	1	Writing Set - silver:	incomplete

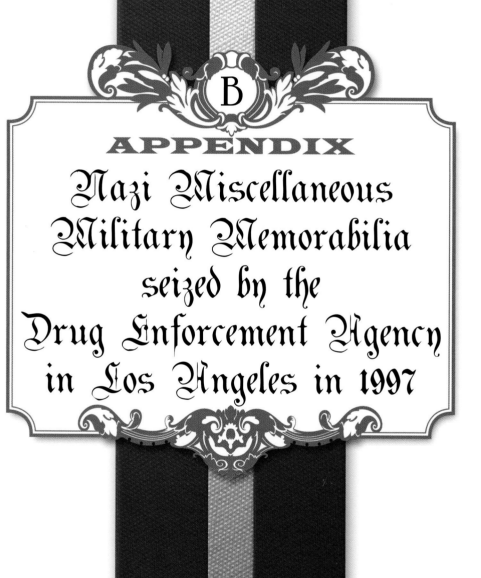

APPENDIX

Nazi Miscellaneous Military Memorabilia seized by the Drug Enforcement Agency in Los Angeles in 1997

DESCRIPTION	ESTIMATES SMITHSONIAN	PRICE FROM SALES INVOICE
97-DEA-333335, Sword Goring Wedding seized 05/29/1997		
1 Sword-yellow Metal W/Eagle & Blk Scabbard-W/ Yellow Metal Tip	$250,000	$2,000,000
97-DEA-333336 seized 05/29/1997 appraisal 05/20/98		
1 1 Hermann Goring's Overcoat and Peaked Visor	50,000	250,000
2 1 Diplomatic Uniform and Overcoat (Ettle's)	3,500	15,000
3 1 Army General's Tunic with Medals (Green)	2,000	3,500
4 1 Von Ribbentrop's Peaked Visor and Medal	15,000	15,000
5 1 NSDAP Reichsleiter's Peaked Visor	2,500	5,000
6 1 Luftwaffe Officer's Peaked Visor – White	2,500	7,500
7 1 Luftwaffe Officer's Peaked Visor – Grey	1,500	7,500
8 1 Aeronautical Research Chain	30,000	150,000
9 1 Oak Leaves and Swords Medal in Case	9,000	25,000
10 1 Oak Leaves Medal in Case	4,500	8,500
11 1 Knights Cross in Case	3,500	3,500
12 1 German Cross - Gold - Brilliants	25,000	35,000
13 1 German Cross - Gold - in Case	1,250	2,500
14 1 German Cross - Silver - in Case	1,750	3,000
15 1 U-Boat Badge - Brilliants and 2 Post Cards	15,000	25,000
16 1 Eagle Orders Ist Class In Case 1 Ribbon	4,000	7,500
17 1 Eagle Order 2nd Class in Case	1,000	1,500
18 1 Golden Party Pin Set	1,250	5,000
19 1 Golden Party Pin	350	500
20 1 Golden Party Pin	350	750
21 2 Hitler Youth Pins	175	450
22 5 Blood Order Group Documents	4,500	25,000
23 1 "SA" High Leader's Dagger	40,000	50,000
24 1 Diplomatic Dagger	9,500	9,500
25 1 Government Official's Dagger and Hanger	8,500	10,000
26 1 Naval Damascus Dagger	4,500	7,500
27 1 Photo of Goring autographed to Malcolm Sanford	3,500	3,500
28 1 NSDAP Reichsleiter Collar Tab	2,000	2,000
29 2 NSDAP Reichsleiter 2 Leaf, 2 Bar Collar Tab	1,500	1,500
30 2 NSDAP Reichsleiter 1 Leaf, 2 Bar Collar Tab	1,250	1,250
31 1 NSDAP Gauleiter Collar Tab	2,000	2,500
32 1 NSDAP Gauleiter 4 Leaf Collar Tab	1,200	1,500
33 2 NSDAP Gauleiter 3 Leaf Bar Collar Tab	1,500	1,500
34 2 NSDAP Gauleiter 3 Leaf Bar Collar Tab	2,000	2,500
35 2 NSDAP Gauleiter 3 Leaf Bar Collar Tab	1,000	1,000

	DESCRIPTION	ESTIMATES SMITHSONIAN	PRICE FROM SALES INVOICE
36	1 NSDAP Gauleiter 2 Leaf Bar Collar Tab	1,250	1,250
37	2 NSDAP Kreis 2 Leaf', 2 Bar Collar Tab	1,250	1,250
38	1 NSDAP Kreis 2 Leaf,l Bar Collar Tab	750	950
39	1 NSDAP Kreis 2 Leaf,l Bar Collar Tab	350	500
40	1 NSDAP Kreis Armband	1,250	1,500
41	1 NSDAP Orts Armband	750	750
42	1 Diplomatic Ost Cuff Title	1,750	2,500
43	1 Luftwaffe Collar Tab Collection, 22 Pairs	2,000	2,000
44	1 Eagle Collection (15 Insignia Badges)	2,750	5,000
45	1 Political Flag	1,500	1,500
46	1 Grand Cross of the Order of the Roman Eagle Ribbon w/Medal	1,500	44,000
47	1 Mannequin & Stand	0	
48	3 Metal Cup, Skill pin & Coffin Box	0	

CHAPTER 1

The photo captions (courtesy of the Library of Congress) are taken from German handwritten notes on the reverse of the photographs.

The photo captions (courtesy of the National Archives) are derived from descriptions on Property Control Cards.

"Hitler has been appointed," Erich Gritzback. *Hermann Göring.* Hurst & Blackett, 1938

Donovan Senter and Ursula Sachs, Alford, Kenneth D. *Allied Looters.* Jefferson, NC: McFarland and Company, 2012

Fraenkel, Heinrich and Manvelle, Roger. *Göring.* Simon and Schuster, New York, 1962

Personal Papers of Mike Morris, Birthday List 1943.

National Archives, Record Group 260, Ardelia Hall, Munich, The gift papers from 1936 through 1940. The train and its contents from Carinhall to Berchtesgaden

I.C.B. Dear. *The Oxford Companion to World War II.* Oxford University Press, New York, 1995

Yeide, Nancy H. *Beyond the Dreams of Avarice.* Dallas: Laurel Publishing, 2009

Alford, Kenneth D. *Hermann Goring and the Nazi Art Collection.* Jefferson, NC: McFarland and Company, 2012

CHAPTER 2

National Archives, Record Group 407 – 3101-4.11, History of the 101st

CHAPTER 3

National Archives, Record Group 407 – 3101-4.11, History of the 101st

CHAPTER 4

1. Hermann J. Giskes, "Operation North Pole." *Reader's Digest*, August, 1953

2. Dear ed, *The Oxford Companion to World War II.*

3. Foreign Military Studies, MS# 636, National Archives.

4. Major General Maxwell D. Taylor, Office of the Division Commander, November 1, 1944.

5. General A. G. McAuliffe, Headquarters 101st Airborne Division, November, 13, 1944.

CHAPTER 5

National Archives, Record Group 407 – 3101-4.11, History of the 101st

CHAPTER 6

National Archives, Record Group 407 – 3101-4.11, History of the 101st

Endnotes

The company clerk for T-Force filed his documents between two pieces of wood. The top photograph is the front with a board and two bolts filed off at the top to sharpen them. The documents are pushed down over the pointed bolts and two nuts applied to hold the file together. Fortunately this file still exists today in the National Archives, and one hopes it remains in its original form. *Courtesy Kenneth D. Alford.*

CHAPTER 7

National Archives, Record Group, 331, G-2 Forces

National Archives, Record Group 407, 1269 Combat Engineer Battalion

From the National Archives – A newspaper clipping of an interview with Willard White's wife. The paper is clipped without a heading or date. It is most likely that the paper is an Austin, Texas, paper and dated during July or August 1945.

1. Thalhofer, Robert L. *Company A!* Xlibris Corporation, 2010

2. Thalhofer, Robert L. *Company A!* Xlibris Corporation, 2010

CHAPTER 8

National Archives, Record Group 407 – 3101-4.11, History of the 101st

1. George Allen, Headquarters 101st Airborne Division, Memorandum for the Officer in Charge, July 12, 1945.

CHAPTER 9

T-Force material, Lt. William J. Owens, Berchtesgaden – the Obersalzberg – 9/12 May 1945 Target No. 2. *The New Yorker*, May 5, 1945.

Hunt, Irmgard A. *On Hitler's Mountain.* New York: William Morrow, 2005

Mitchell, Arthur H. *Hitler's Mountain.*

White/Johnson story regarding the Luger from Ben Curtis Email.

1. Harry Sions: *Yank*, May 1945.

2. Harry Sions: *Yank*, May 1945.

CHAPTER 10

The two batons – Approximately 50 pages of the army's investigation in 1946/47, Civil Affairs, National Archives, and Kenneth Alford's collection.

101st Airborne enters Berchtesgaden one day after the 101st, Rapport and Norwood. *Rendezvous with History.* page 732.

Record Group 331 T-Force, Headquarters Sixth Army Group.

Number of inventory items moved to Munich Central Collection Center from the Thomas Carr Howe Jr. Collection, The Archives of American Art, Handwritten page Recapitulation.

http://www.lostart.de/Content/04_Datenbank/EN/RestbestandCCP.html?nn=7482

Howe, Thomas Carr Jr. *Salt Mines and Castles.* The Bobbs-Merrill Company, New York, 1946.

McManus, John C. *The Eagle's Nest: The last Great Prize.* World War II. May 2005.

Rapport and Norwood. *Rendezvous with History.* Old Saybrook: Konecky & Konecky, 1948.

Rorimer, James J. Survival: *The Salvage and Protection of Art in War.* New York: Abelard Press, 1950.

Major E.U. McRae involvement – Daily Dairy, 30 May 1945, Wednesday; Pratt Museum, Fort Campbell, Kentucky.

Information regarding Edward S. Peck, Harry V. Anderson; "To Whom It May Concern," August 5, 1945.

References to origin of porcelain, Ducret, S. *German Porcelain*: New York: Universal Book, 1962.

1. Harry Anderson, an undated, unsigned letter to Agnes Mongan.

2. Gorge Allen, Hermann Göring, Guard's Eye View, July 25, 1945.

3. Robert L Thalhofer, Company A, and dates from Daily Dairy, 30 May 1945, Wednesday. Pratt Museum, Fort Campbell, Kentucky.

4. Ardelia Hall, Memorandum of Conversation, March 3, 1954.

CHAPTER 11

Ben Curtis recall is from an email of Friday, 8/26/2011.

Miss Patricia Hartwell, from the Telegraph News, March 29, 2007.

CHAPTER 13

www.antique-china-porcelain-collection and Eriken, Svend. *Sèvres Porcelain*. Faber and Faber, Boston, 1987

CHAPTER 14

1. J.S. Plaut, Consolidated Interrogation Report no. 2, activity of Einsatzstab Rosenberg in France, August 15, 1945.

CHAPTER 16

With the 101st Airborne Division in Auxerre, France, September 6, 1945.

Headquarters – 101st Airborne Division, Public Relations Office, September 1, 1945.

George Maley, "The Extraordinary Life of the Blue Goose."

CHAPTER 17

Angolia, Major John R., "Daggers, Bayonets & Fighting Knives of Hitler's Germany". Mountain View, California, R. James Bender Publishing Co., 1971.

Angolia, Major John R., "Edged Weaponry of the Third Reich," Mountain View, California, R. James Bender Publishing Co., 1974.

Atwood, Major James P., "The Daggers and Edged Weapons of Hitler's Germany," Berlin, Germany, Omnium-Druck and Verlag, 1965.

Atwood, Major James P., "World War II Treasure Hunt for Hitler's Daggers of Glory," SAGA (Vol. 34, No. 2) May, 1967, p. 8.

Johnson, Thomas M., "Collecting the Edged Weapons of the Third Reich, Volume I," Columbia, South Carolina, The R.L. Bryan Co., 1975.

Johnson, Thomas M., "Collecting the Edged Weapons of the Third Reich, Volume III," Columbia, South Carolina, The R.L. Bryan Co., 1978.

Johnson, Thomas M., "Collecting the Edged Weapons of the Third Reich, Volume IV," Columbia, South Carolina, The R.L. Bryan Co., 1981.

Life Magazine, June 11, 1945.

New York Times, May 21, 1945.

Thalhofer, Robert L., "Company A! Combat Engineers Remember World War II." Xlibris Corporation, 2010.

CHAPTER 18

Interrogations of Emmy Göring by E.E. Minskoff, October 1945.

Interrogations of Emmy Göring, Office of the Inspector General, September 1945.

"Project Millennium, Airmen of Courage our Heritage"; an Interview with Colonel William Stewart, USAF (Ret) 1 October 2004.

L.A. 54/42 & L.A. 54/44, Washington Historical Society, July 20 and July 23, 1954.

Letter to Colonel William F. Stewart from Chapin D. Foster, April 1, 1958.

Letter to Chapin D. Foster from William F. Steward, April 2, 1958.

"Some Time Ago," *The News Tribune*, Tacoma, WA, February 23, 1979.

"To Whom It May Concern" from Colonel William Stewart, February 26, 1979.

Emmy Göring. *My life with Göring.* London, David Bruce & Watson, 1972.

Ben Curtis emails, November 22, 2011 and March 1, 2012.

U.S. Marshals Service: The source organization is documented as Dept of Justice, U.S. Marshals Service, U.S. Court House, 312 North Spring Street, Los Angeles, CA.

U.S. Marshals Service, FOI 2012USMS19025 filed by Kenneth D. Alford, received May 2, 2012.

The source material used to prepare this study was largely obtained from manuscript documents that are listed under notes for each specific entry. The titles listed below were also used, largely for general background information.

Akinsha, Konstantin, and Grigorii Kozlov. *Beautiful Loot: The Soviet Plunder of Europe's Art Treasures*. New York: Random House, 1995

Alford, Kenneth D. *The Spoils of World War II*. New York: Birch Lane Press, 1994 – *Great Treasure Stories of World War II*. Mason City, Iowa: Savas Publishing Company, 2000 – *Nazi Millionaires*. Haverty, Pa.: Casemate, 2002

Alford, Kenneth D. *Hermann Göring and the Nazi Art Collection*. Jefferson , N.C.:McFarland and Company, 2012

Alford, Kenneth D. *Allied Looting in World War II*. Jefferson, N.C.: McFarland and Company, 2012

Ambrose, Stephen E. *Band of Brothers*. New York: Simon & Schuster, 1992

Bradley, Omar N. *A Soldier's Story*. New York: Holt and Company, 1951

Bradley, Omar N., and Clay Blair. *A General's Life: An Autobiography by General of the Army Omar N. Bradley*. New York: Simon and Schuster, 1983.

Butcher, Harry C. *My Three Years with Eisenhower: The Personal Diary of Captain Harry C. Butcher, USNR, Naval Aide to General Eisenhower, 1942-1945*. New York: Simon and Schuster, 1946.

D'Este, Carlo. *Patton: A Genius for War*. New York: HarperCollins, 1995. ———. *Eisenhower: A Soldier's Life*. New York: Henry Holt, 2002.

Duberman, Martin. *The Worlds of Lincoln Kirstein*. New York: Alfed A. Knopf, 2007.

Ducret, S. *German Porcelain*: New York: Universal Book, 1962

Edsel, Robert M. *Rescuing Da Vinci: Hitler and the Nazis Stole Europe's Great Art, America and Her Allies Recovered It*. Dallas: Laurel Publishing, 2006.

Eisenhower, Dwight D. *Crusade in Europe*. New York: Doubleday & Co., 1948. Eriken, Svend. *Sèvres Porcelain*. Boston: Faber and Faber, 1987

Flanner, Janet. *Men and Monuments*. New York: Harper & Brothers, 1957.

Göring, Emmy. *My Life with Göring*. London: David Bruce & Watson, 1972

Harrison, C.A. *Cross Channel Attack*. Washington D.C.: U S Government Printing Office, 1951

Hitler, Adolf. *Mein Kampf*. Translated by Ralph Manheim. New York: Houghton Mifflin, 1943.

Holladay, Joan A. *Illuminating the Epic*. Seattle: University of Washington Press, 1996

Howe, Thomas Carr Jr. *Salt Mines and Castles*: The Bobbs-Merrill Company, New York, 1946

Hunt, Irmgard A. *On Hitler's Mountain*. New York: William Morrow, 2005

Konstantine Akinsha and Grigorii Kazlov. *Beautiful Loot*. New York: Random House, 1995

Kurtz, Michael J. *America and the Return of Nazi Contraband: The Recovery of Europe's Cultural Treasures*. Cambridge, UK: Cambridge University Press, 2006.

McDonald, Charles B. *The last Offensive*. United States Army, Washington D.C: 1984

Mitchell, Arthur H. *Hitler's Mountain*.

Mosley, Leonard. *The Reich Marshal*. New York: Doubleday & Company, 1974

Nazi Conspiracy and Aggression. Washington, DC: U.S. Government Printing Office, 1946.

Nicholas, Lynn. *The Rape of Europa*. New York: Vintage, 1995.

Nuremberg 14 November 1945 – 1 October 1946. Nuremberg: International Military Tribunal, 1947.

Rapport and Norwood. *Rendezvous with History*. Old Saybrook: Konecky & Konecky, 1948

Report of the American Commission for the Protection and Salvage of Artistic and Historic Monuments in War Areas. Washington, DC: U.S. Government Printing Office, 1946.

Rorimer, James J. *Survival: The Salvage and Protection of Art in War*. New York: Abelard Press, 1950.

Shirer, William L. *Berlin Diary: The Journal of a Foreign Correspondent: 1934–1941*. Norwalk, CT: The Easton Press, 1991. - *The Rise and Fall of the Third Reich: A History of Nazi Germany*. Norwalk, CT: The Easton Press, 1991.

Smyth, Craig Hugh. *Repatriation of Art from the Collecting Point in Munich after World War II*. New Jersey: Abner Schram Ltd., 1988.

Speer, Albert. *Inside the Third Reich*. New York: Macmillan, 1970.

Stanton, Shelby l. *World War II Order of Battle*. New York: Galahad Books, 1984

Trial of the Major War Criminals before the International Military Tribunal:

Thalhofer, Robert L. *Company A!*. Xlibris Corporation, 2010

Wynne, Frank. *I Was Vermeer*. New York: Bloombury, 2006

Yeide, Nancy H. *Beyond the Dream of Avarice*. Dallas: Laurel Publishing, 2009

Index